Women Judges

Do women have equal chances in the judiciary? Although women have made their way into law faculties, in many countries of the world they still face drawbacks in judicial careers. This book delves into the different aspects of women at work in the judicial environment, focusing on judicial appointments, promotions, the glass ceiling, and representation in high positions of the judiciary across international settings such as Nigeria, South Africa, Philippines, Turkey, Spain, and Northern Ireland. The contributions go beyond the classical career issues by digging into several questions related to women at work in the judicial environment, such as: Are women accepted by their colleagues and by clients at court – male and female? Do they get the recognition they deserve or is there indecent behaviour and discrimination against them? What about work–life balance? And how do women judges perceive their role?

The book offers valuable insights by questioning and criticising the status quo, paving the way to a gender equal future in the judiciary. A significant new contribution to international scholarship in the field, this book was originally published as a special issue of the *International Journal of the Legal Profession.*

Ulrike Schultz is a retired senior academic of FernUniversität in Hagen, Germany, specialised in the sociology of the legal professions, legal education, questions of gender and law. She has taken part in and organised many international socio-legal projects. She was President of the Research Committee for the Sociology of Law 2018–2023.

Tabeth Masengu is a human rights lawyer and socio-legal researcher. Her areas of research include the rule of law, gender and judging, governance in Africa, Constitutionalism, human rights, policy reform, and intersectional discrimination.

Avrom Sherr is Emeritus Professor at the Institute of Advanced Legal Studies in the United Kingdom. He leads the quality assurance of legal aid lawyers in England and Wales. He is the founding editor of the *International Journal of the Legal Profession.*

Women Judges

Women Judges

Appointments, Career Chances and Barriers

Edited by
Ulrike Schultz, Tabeth Masengu and Avrom Sherr

Routledge
Taylor & Francis Group
LONDON AND NEW YORK

First published 2024
by Routledge
4 Park Square, Milton Park, Abingdon, Oxon OX14 4RN

and by Routledge
605 Third Avenue, New York, NY 10158

Routledge is an imprint of the Taylor & Francis Group, an informa business

British Library Cataloguing in Publication Data
A catalogue record for this book is available from the British Library

ISBN13: 978-1-032-73623-5 (hbk)
ISBN13: 978-1-032-73625-9 (pbk)
ISBN13: 978-1-003-46514-0 (ebk)

DOI: 10.4324/9781003465140

Typeset in Minion Pro
by Newgen Publishing UK

Publisher's Note
The publisher accepts responsibility for any inconsistencies that may have arisen during the conversion of this book from journal articles to book chapters, namely the inclusion of journal terminology.

Disclaimer
Every effort has been made to contact copyright holders for their permission to reprint material in this book. The publishers would be grateful to hear from any copyright holder who is not here acknowledged and will undertake to rectify any errors or omissions in future editions of this book.

Contents

Citation Information

The chapters in this book were originally published in the *International Journal of the Legal Profession*, volume 27, issue 2 (2020). When citing this material, please use the original page numbering for each article, as follows:

Introduction

Women and judicial appointments
Ulrike Schultz and Tabeth Masengu
International Journal of the Legal Profession, volume 27, issue 2 (2020), pp. 113–117

Chapter 1

Being a woman judge in Turkish judicial culture
Seda Kalem
International Journal of the Legal Profession, volume 27, issue 2 (2020), pp. 119–144

Chapter 2

A five-year gender equality score card for the Philippine Supreme Court under its first woman Chief Justice: opportunities seized and missed
Emily Sanchez Salcedo
International Journal of the Legal Profession, volume 27, issue 2 (2020), pp. 145–159

Chapter 3

The Judicial Service Commission and the appointment of women: more to it than meets the eye
Tabeth Masengu
International Journal of the Legal Profession, volume 27, issue 2 (2020), pp. 161–174

Chapter 4

Women in the Nigerian judiciary: considerable headway or organised progress?
Enibokun Uzebu-Imarhiagbe
International Journal of the Legal Profession, volume 27, issue 2 (2020), pp. 175–188

Chapter 5

The glass ceiling at the highest levels of the Spanish judiciary
Mónica García Goldar
International Journal of the Legal Profession, volume 27, issue 2 (2020), pp. 189–202

Chapter 6

Problems in the pathways to judicial success: women in the legal profession in Northern Ireland
Leah Treanor
International Journal of the Legal Profession, volume 27, issue 2 (2020), pp. 203–216

Notes on Contributors

Mónica García Goldar, Civil Law Department, University of Santiago de Compostela, Santiago de Compostela, Spain.

Seda Kalem, Istanbul Bilgi University Faculty of Law.

Tabeth Masengu, human rights lawyer and socio-legal researcher.

Emily Sanchez Salcedo, Commercial Law Department, De La Salle University, Manila, Philippines.

Ulrike Schultz, FernUniversität in Hagen, Germany.

Avrom Sherr, Institute of Advanced Legal Studies, UK.

Leah Treanor, School of Law, Queen's University Belfast, Belfast, UK.

Enibokun Uzebu-Imarhiagbe, Department of History and International Studies, University of Benin, Benin City, Edo State, Nigeria.

Introduction: women and judicial appointments

The six papers in this special issue deal with various aspects of women in the judiciary in six different countries: two contributions are from sub-Saharan Africa: South Africa and Nigeria, two from Europe: Northern Ireland and Spain and two from very different parts of Asia: Turkey and the Philippines. The papers on Africa and Europe have been presented at an Expert Seminar on Gender and the Judiciary organised by Tabeth Masengu under the auspices of the Human Rights Centre at Ghent University in Belgium on the 27th of April 2018. The two papers on Asia have been developed in the context of a project on Women Judges in Muslim Courts of Law which was an International Research Collaborative for the international socio-legal meeting in Mexico-City in 2017.

Adding new countries, this special issue of the International Journal of the Legal Profession complements other international comparative collections on gender issues in the judiciary which have been published in the past years. These include the comprehensive volume with 30 contributions on 19 countries "Gender and Judging" (Schultz and Shaw 2013a), two special issues of the International Journal of the Legal Profession "Women in the Judiciary" (Schultz and Shaw 2012), and "Gender and Judicial Education" (Schultz *et al.* 2016); and a collection on "Women Judges in the Muslim World" (Lindbekk and Sonneveld 2017) as well as an upcoming issue of the Onati Socio-Legal Online Series on Gender in Muslim courts of Law. National publications are innumerable and still new research projects on related issues are launched, e.g. at the University of Bergen/ Norway on "Women on the Bench. The Role of Female Judges in Fragile States".[1] Also documentary films on women judges have been produced: e.g. on Ruth Bader Ginsberg, the feminist judge at the American Supreme Court, "RBG" and "On the Basis of Sex" (both 2018), "The Judge" (2018) about the first female Sharía Court judge in Palestine, "Lady Judges in Pakistan" (2013) by Livia and Marius Holden, "Courting Justice" (2010) by Ruth Cowan about Women Judges in South Africa after Apartheid,[2] "Sisters in Law" (2005) about women judges in Kameron.

A broad range of subjects related to women in the judiciary are covered in all the mentioned publications. These include topics such as access and careers in the judiciary, dealing with the question: Do women have equal chances in the judiciary, do they have equal representation in higher positions or do they hit the famous glass ceiling? Are they accepted by their colleagues and by clients at court, male and female clients? Is there indecent behaviour and/or discrimination against female judges?

Is it easy or particularly difficult for women in the judiciary to find a work/family-life balance? What are impeding factors? What are the prevailing gender images in their societies? Is there a relation between participation of women in the judiciary and prestige and pay?

Do women judge differently? In what way may gender, age, marital-parental status, position and race/ethnicity influence their decision making (and of course that of their male counterparts)? Can class or other differences in background create a divide between the elite women judges and the "ordinary" women taking their cases to court? Do women judges have a more caring attitude to clients? What are the expectations from people at court towards female judges?

What do the women judges perceive as their role: Do they contribute in impowering women in their rights, also customary or indigenous rights through the court system?

Women had been excluded from taking law degrees, entering practice as lawyers and being admitted to the judiciary in most countries till the beginning, in some countries till well into the 20th century, even in Europe: in France in 1946, in the Netherlands 1947, in Italy in 1965, in Portugal in 1978. In these countries they have caught up fast and are in the majority now. In India and China however where it would not be expected, the first women were admitted to the judiciary as early as 1926. In many Arab countries, admissions occurred only in the last two decades or even the last few years often due to pressure of donor countries. In Kuwait there is no female judge even today (2020), and in Iran none left. The Nobel Peace Prize winner Shirin Ebadi was the first and so far only female judge in Iran from 1975 to 1979. (Schultz 2021) Low numbers of female judges are in some fragile states, e.g. in Afghanistan (11%) and Haiti (10%). The number of judges in these states is dependent on influences of the political system, whether there is a more authoritarian, conservative or a more socialist, communist regime, the influence of the former colonial systems and partly also religion.

In many countries women judges are meanwhile in the majority, however often still underrepresented in leading positions. Data for Europe can be found at the website of the European Institute for Gender Equality (EIGE),[3] at the website of the United Nations Economic Commission for Europe "Share of women among judges in Europe 2017"[4]; at the OECD website (for 2017),[5] also in "European Parliament" (2017); for the USA at the website of the National Association of Women Judges,[6] for Latin America and the Caribbean from the Gender Equality Observatory,[7] just to give examples.

The type of legal systems matters in selection methods: is it a common law or civil law system, is it based on or blended with Islamic, as well as Asian and African legal traditions? Are there career judges who enter the judiciary at a young age, or are judges nominated on professional merit at an older age?

In the case of career judges competitive examinations work in favour of women, on the upper levels of the judiciary gate keeping is stronger: In almost all countries the way in which positions of power are accessed and enacted is gendered which means that besides formal there are informal obstacles which are difficult to grasp. Networks are often closed to women, their own women's networks are often less strong and assertive than the traditional men's networks. Political affiliation and kinship networks may matter. Interesting differences have been described for many countries between practice in the big cities and in the countryside, in some states a career as a judge means to move around in a country which makes it difficult for women to combine family and work. We hear of women who complain the heavy workload they have to master, that they are expected to be "asexual" beings, but women judges have an overall high job satisfaction.

In many countries there is besides the vertical stratification a horizontal one, women refined to family courts, in others family matters are part of the religious / Sharía courts jurisdiction which is in most cases reserved to men. In some countries, e.g. Afghanistan horizontal stratification takes the form of a gender-segregated system.

There is some evidence that women approach judging differently, e.g. in investigative matters, how they handle victims and witnesses in procedure, that their style of communication may differ, as well as their style of writing judgments, and the perception and the reception of their judicial opinions may differ.[8] Women may also come to different results. The question if women judge differently has been dealt with in numerous publications as well as theoretical concepts from gender difference theory over individualistic approaches to a deconstruction of gender (Schultz 2016, 2017, 2020; Schultz and Shaw 2013b). There is evidence that in some countries the competence and authority of women judges is more likely to be questioned and they are seen less likely to be impartial, although it is a hard empirical fact from different countries that women judges are less prone to bribery and corruption.[9] An explanation can be that they often are not the main breadwinners of the family, the question however remains whether they are more "virtuous" than men maybe due to a gendered education.

There are still questions to be dealt with: Intersectional discrimination judges experience, at the interface of gender, sexual orientation, age, marital-parental status and race/ethnicity still deserves a closer look in many countries. What about judges in countries where e.g. homosexuality is forbidden by death penalty? In Germany a judge at the Supreme Court underwent a sex change a couple of years ago which only got a few remarks in the press, as officially we hold everyone in high esteem and do not discriminate – but unofficially? Whatever the share of women in the judiciary is, training in gender issues is important for women and men to reflect their own position and the work they do to be able to do justice to all genders and sexes to the best of their abilities, and pave the way to an elimination of discrimination (Schultz 2014).

To the contributions in this issue:

Based on interviews Seda Kalem deals in her contribution "Being a Woman Judge in Turkish Judicial Culture" with the life realities of female judges in her country: with their work in a profession which is considered to be masculine and with their social lives which confronts them with classical expectations as women, wives and mothers. Although 47% of the judges are women, the judicial reform strategy paper from 2019 set the goal to maintain gender equality in personnel recruitment,[10] the interviews have revealed a prevalence of a particularly conservative and patriarchal culture. Judges live apart from society, independence of judges is understood as not being in touch with society at large. Women are often confined to their homes with few professional contacts and network opportunities. Focussed on their professional tasks, which they all considered as very demanding, the judges were however hardly aware of the working of gender in their professional development and in spite of the high percentage of women there is a marked re-traditionalization of the image of a judge.

Emily Sanchez-Salcedo evaluates in her chapter the impact of the first woman appointed Chief Justice of the Philippine Supreme Court. First and early women in leading judicial positions are always confronted with the expectation to improve the judicial product towards gender equality. Analysing the judgments in which Maria Lourdes Sereno was involved, the author draws a mixed balance. Sereno who could only serve a limited time of office had a delicate task. In some decisions involving important women's issues, she was able to make a difference, in others she was not successful. The author concludes that a much needed push for women's issues was given, that opportunities had been seized, but others missed and therefore opportunities for greater gender equality had been lost.

The following four papers focus on women's appointment to the judiciary by highlighting women's careers and obstacles.

Tabeth Masengu hones in on the workings of the appointing body in South Africa, in her chapter "The Judicial Service Commission in South Africa and the appointment of women: more to it than meets the eye". Her paper employs data from interview participants including judges, lawyers, judicial appointers, journalists and members of Civil Society organisations. It also incorporates data from participant observation of the judicial appointment interviews between 2013 and 2017 and workshops with judges and lawyers. She challenges the notion that using judicial appointment bodies negates the patronage and partiality that was previously present in executive only appointments. This is especially important because the majority of Commonwealth countries have done away with appointments made solely by the executive and literature argues that this move has resulted in a fairer and more transparent appointment process. The paper identifies three sites of partiality, power and patronage as observed in the JSC process– specifically regarding the appointment of women. These are in the form of the presence of politics in interviews, patronage in required criteria and partiality in the recruitment of judges. It concludes by advising that if the identified issues are not addressed, the advantages of appointment bodies as opposed to executive type appointments will start to diminish.

The contribution from Enibokun Uzebu-Imarhiagbe is a historical account of women judges in Mid-Western Nigeria. Entitled "Women in the Nigerian Judiciary: Considerable Headway or Organised Progress?", this paper uses qualitative empirical data from interviews with judges and information gleaned from government records and personal files of judges in the archives of the judiciaries in Edo and Delta states in Mid-Western Nigeria. The increase of women in the High Court division is attributed to the selection of judicial candidates from the magistracy and government departments where many female practitioners are employed. While jobs in these fields of the public service have less financial remuneration than private practice, she argues that the regular hours proved more conducive for women. Uzebu-Imarhiagbe concludes that women's progression to judgeship on the High Court, resulted from the judiciary's need for qualified legal practitioners, regardless of gender, thus, creating a history of reception and advancement for women candidates, rather than exclusion.

Mónica García Goldar's paper "The Glass Ceilings at the Highest Levels of the Spanish Judiciary" notes the contradiction between government supported Strategic Plans for Equity and the low number of women judges in Spain's highest judiciaries. Despite the series of measures included in the Strategic Plans for Equality in the Judicial Career (2013 and 2020), Garcia Goldar submits that the glass ceiling for women in Spain appears to be unbreakable and refers to statistics on Spain's highest courts to make the point. The Constitutional Court only has a 17% composition of women and there are no women on the Spanish Supreme Court. The paper describes the evolution of the presence of women in the Spanish judiciary and also suggests some of the possible causes for the glass ceiling. Referring to comparative data in other European countries, the paper emphasises that the glass ceiling is also present in other European countries although there are differences in respect of the patterns of representation. Garcia Goldar concludes by offering three possible solutions that could alleviate the identified problem in Spain.

Leah Treanor's paper on "Problems in the pathways to judicial success: women in the legal profession in Northern Ireland" sheds light on the under-explored situation of women in the judiciary in Northern Ireland. Using a critical, social constructionist feminist approach, this contribution explores some of the gendered barriers influencing women's under-representation in order to assess future judicial gender parity prospects in this jurisdiction. The paper analyses the eligibility requirements for judges, the interactions of merit and gender in the work of the Northern Ireland Judicial Appointment Commission, gendered occupational segregation and the "motherhood penalty".

It is emphasised that the representation of women in the judiciary can only be improved when women's retention and progression through the ranks of the legal profession in Northern Ireland is addressed.

Notes

1. https://www.cmi.no/projects/2122-women-on-the-bench.
2. https://www.courtingjustice.com/.

3. On highest and supreme courts https://eige.europa.eu/gender-statistics/dgs/browse/wmidm/wmidm_jud/wmidm_jud_natcrt.
4. https://w3.unece.org/PXWeb/en/DataMap?IndicatorCode=32.
5. https://www.oecd.org/gender/data/women-in-the-judiciary-working-towards-a-legal-system-reflective-of-society.htm data for Germany however incomplete.
6. https://www.nawj.org/statistics.
7. https://oig.cepal.org/en/indicators/judicial-power-percentage-women-judges-highest-court-or-supreme-court.
8. Current research by Nina Varsava, University of Wisconsin-Madison.
9. General data on corruption in the judiciary: Survey on the Independence of Judges 2016/17 www.encj.eu.
10. https://www.hurriyetdailynews.com/number-of-female-judges-and-prosecutors-in-turkey-at-its-highest-143963.

References

European Parliament. (2017) *Mapping the representation of women and men in legal professions across the EU.* I was one of the authors. Available at: https://www.europarl.europa.eu/RegData/etudes/STUD/2017/596804/IPOL_STU(2017)596804_EN.pdf.

Lindbekk, M. & Sonneveld, N. (Eds) (2017) *Women Judges in the Muslim World* (Leiden, Brill).

Schultz, U. (2014) Raising gender awareness of judges – elements for judicial education in Germany, *International Journal of the Legal Profession, Special Issue on Gender and Judicial Education*, 3, pp. 345–355.

Schultz, U. (2016) Sexism in law and the impact of gender stereotypes in legal proceedings, in: Heinrich Boell Stiftung South Caucasus (Ed) *Fight for the Public Space: When Personal is Political (Tiflis)*, pp. 97–108. Available at: https://ge.boell.org/en/2016/12/29/fight-public-space-when-private-political.

Schultz, U. (2017) Do female judges judge better? in: N. Sonneveld & M. Lindbekk (Eds) *Women Judges in the Muslim World* (Leiden, Brill), pp. 23–50.

Schultz, U. (2020) Gender and its impact on decision-making in (international) arbitration. A view from Germany, *International Journal of the Legal Profession* (forthcoming).

Schultz, U. (2021) Introduction: gender and careers in the legal academy: overview and synthesis, in: U. Schultz, G. Shaw, M. Thornton & R. Auchmuty (Eds) *Gender and Careers in the Legal Academy* (Oxford, Hart).

Schultz, U. & Shaw, G. (Eds) (2012) *Women in the Judiciary* (London, New York, Routledge) (reprint of special issue *Gender and Judging* International Journal of the Legal Profession, Volume 15, numbers 1–2, March–July 2008).

Schultz, U. & Shaw, G. (Eds) (2013a) *Gender and Judging* (Oxford, Hart).

Schultz, U. & Shaw, G. (2013b) Introduction: gender and judging: overview and synthesis, in: U. Schultz & G. Shaw (Eds) *Gender and Judging* (Oxford, Hart), pp. 3–47.

Schultz, U., Shaw, G. & Dawson, B. (Eds) (2016) *Gender and Judicial Education* (London, New York, Routledge) (reprint of special issue *Gender and Judicial Education* International Journal of the Legal Profession, Volume 21, number 3, November 2014, and parts of Volume 22, number 2, July 2015).

Ulrike Schultz
Tabeth Masengu

Being a woman judge in Turkish judicial culture

Seda Kalem

ABSTRACT

This study is a feminist exploration of how gender influences the professional and social lives of women judges in Turkey. I asked women judges from lower courts to talk about their professional journey to explore if and how gender emerges as a category that makes sense to them. Gender was sometimes more visible in the form of a "success" story of playing along men's rules, or in memories of struggling to balance work and family; while other times it was more implicit in narratives on meeting expectations, failing expectations, ignoring expectations. All in all, these narratives attest to the gendered hierarchies and instances of institutional sexism in what is considered a masculine profession. They also reveal the prevalence of a particularly conservative and patriarchal culture upon the ways in which these inequalities and disadvantages are experienced by women judges in Turkey.

1. Introduction: why study women judges in Turkey?

Women in Turkey have been on the bench since the early 1920s and in increasing numbers. Women judges constitute 47% of the total number of judges in Turkey as of 2019. In that sense, the judiciary, like the legal profession, seems like a field with relative gender equality. Numbers, however, can be misleading on their own. Data also reveal that there is significant vertical segregation in the legal field with women facing strong glass ceilings while trying to advance in their careers. There is also an extension of gender roles in the form of horizontal segregation where women get to occupy positions that are socially and culturally considered more appropriate for them. One defining factor in these institutionalized distinctions is the role of women in the family. The pervasive gendered division of labor in the social order delegates domestic responsibilities - including household as well as childcare - predominantly to women. Hence, while trying to step up the professional ladder, or practice in areas of law that are considered as more prestigious or when they aspire to be a prosecutor, women in the judiciary are more likely to come across invisible yet highly obstructive barriers.

Studying the situation of women judges in Turkey is also important for a contextualization of gender in the professional field. With the founding of the new Republic in 1923, women in Turkey were granted significant civil and political rights. The new Republic considered women's legal emancipation and their equal presence in public life alongside with men to be one of the most obvious indicators of the new modernizing nation. Particularly in the first couple of decades of the new regime, women were encouraged by the new secular State and its elite men to get higher education and become professionals in many diverse fields (Acar, 1998, p. 321; Ülgen and Ongun, 2010, p. 68). Despite her newfound presence in the public sphere, however, this woman was primarily to assume the fundamental responsibility of raising a family with Republican values. Balım-Harding argues that since women were "given all the rights that they could possibly hope for", all they were expected to do was to "consolidate their traditional roles as daughters, sisters, wives and mothers with their roles as educated, asexual, sober professionals" (1999, p. 112).

In light of this historical and ideological background, starting with the late 1980s the emergence of an organized women's movement has led to a considerable amount of feminist work on women in public life in Turkey with a particular attention to the impact of the regime upon women's presence in the workforce. As opposed to the early feminists who were ardent supporters of the new regime's aspirations for women, these critical feminists pointed out to the instrumental nature of these reforms that considered women's emancipation as a means for the modernization of the whole nation rather than as an end on its own. They particularly drew attention to the class dimension of the reforms – mainly targeting elite, urban women-, as well as to their conservative nature that prioritized women's role in the new family over their equal participation in public life (Kandiyoti, 1987, p. 323). Within this context, women academics (Acar, 1998; Tepe, 2018), executives (Kabasakal, 1998), politicians (Arat, 1989; Güneş-Ayata, 1998) have all been studied from a critical perspective which entailed not merely recognizing the merits of the Republic for women's empowerment but also questioning its transformative power.

Despite a growing literature on women judges all around the world however, in Turkey the issue has not aroused a comparable interest among scholars, researchers, or even within the feminist movement itself.[1] There is also a quite limited number of pieces written by women judges in practice, on being a woman judge in Turkish judiciary especially in relation to the burden of cultural and social pressures (Bülbül, 2015; Köksal, 2015). This absence also has to do with the fact that feminist legal research in Turkey has been confined to issues of the gendered nature of law and legal decisions and how the law and the judicial system treats women with a specific focus on issues of violence (Akyüz *et al.*, 2014; *Ankara Barosu Dergisi*, 2015; Uygur and Özdemir, 2018).

This study then aims to present a critical feminist exploration of what it means to be a woman judge in Turkish judicial culture. For this purpose, in the period of December 2015–April 2016, I conducted seven interviews with women judges from different courts in Istanbul and Ankara. The intended sample was in fact twenty judges who were to be reached through personal and professional networks as well as snowballing; however, following the failed coup attempt against the government and the President on 15 July 2016, I had to exit the field. Immediately after the attempt, a nationwide state of emergency was declared that lasted for two years and presidential decrees passed during this period further consolidated the power of the executive. The failed coup also caused a major crackdown in the judiciary with 2,745 judges and prosecutors immediately being dismissed from the profession the day after the attempt. The purge has left a highly damaged judicial apparatus, with significant wounds on its merits-based system and a growing skepticism around its independence. Hence, during such political and social upheavals with direct consequences upon the judiciary and more specifically upon their professional security, skepticism – fueled with a seemingly effective institution of denunciation among colleagues – became the common approach among judges towards any exploration regarding their work.[2]

I do keep the hope of going back to continue with my study and even expand it to include women prosecutors for a more comprehensive exploration of how gender is constructed, experienced and performed in different professions in the judiciary. In addition, the existing research is confined with stories of quite senior judges with an average professional experience of 28 years. It would also be interesting to look into experiences of younger generation of women judges in order to track similarities and differences between gender narratives. This is also important in the context of the dominant political and ideological turn in Turkey in the last two decades. The growing political and social conservatism in Turkey under the rule of *Adalet ve Kalkınma Partisi* (Justice and Development Party-AKP) has presented itself most vividly in issues relating to gender equality. The ruling party has increasingly assumed a "religio-conservative" position in social issues and redefined womanhood and motherhood in reference to "religion, tradition and custom" which are already treasured values in this conservative and highly patriarchal society (Güneş-Ayata and Doğangün, 2017). Hence it would be interesting to see if and how this new "gender climate" can be traced in the ways in which younger judges talk about being a woman in the judiciary (Cindoğlu and Ünal, 2017). At the same time, a more updated study could also investigate the possible changes introduced by feminization of the judiciary such as emerging issues and new strategies developed women judges.

2. Modernization, professionalization and women judges in Turkey

After the fall of the Ottomon Empire at the end of WW1 and the following War of Independence, the Republic of Turkey was founded in 1923. With the ambition of situating the new Republic as the modern and the progressive vis-à-vis the allegedly backward and traditional Empire, in light of the ideals of the new regime the entire legal landscape went through significant transformations in the 1920s and the 1930s. Beginning with the abolition of the Sultanate in 1922 and the Caliphate in 1924, Republican elites initiated a phase of speedy legal reforms towards secularization of the state with massive effects upon the social life. These measures were all reflexive of a political project that considered the idea of "becoming western" as an end in itself. This was at the same time an ideological reconstruction of the society through comprehensive legal reform that imagined a new type of social living.

In this politico-cultural setting, reforms for improving women's status in public life were considered to be particularly important for the development of a modern and *laïc* nation.[3] It was important for the new state to increase the public visibility of women as a clear indicator of its demarcation with the Ottoman past. The Republican elites have therefore instigated a radical judicial reform that included giving unprecedented rights and freedoms to women in public life. In 1924, with the Law on the Unification of Education, for the first time women and men were provided with equal educational opportunities. With the adoption of the Swiss Civil Code in 1926, polygamy was made illegal and both parties were granted with equal rights on matters of divorce and inheritance. In 1930 and 1934, women of the Republic were also given political rights to elect and be elected in local and national elections. Educated women of the new regime were also encouraged to become whoever they wanted to be: a pilot, an engineer, a parliamentarian, a medical doctor, a judge. And so, they did. In the legal field, for instance, women were enrolled in a law faculty as early as 1921 even before the Republic of Turkey was officially founded. During the 1921–1922 academic year, Istanbul Darülfünun, the first and the only university founded in 1921, had 67 students with four of them being women (Balcı, 2018, p. 80). As for the bench, the first woman judge of the new Republic was notably Suat Berk who was assigned to a Civil Court of Peace in 1925.[4]

Nonetheless, Kemalist[5] regime's instrumental take on the modernization of women as a symbol of the new nation's appropriation of western values has been criticized for creating an ideal image of the Republican woman who was expected above all to serve the interests of the new regime (Tekeli, 1982). These "emancipated but unliberated" women, however, continued to be main bearers of a masculine public morality founded upon the sacredness of women's sexuality (Kandiyoti, 1987). Hence, this "state feminism" (White, 2003) that aspired to change the outlook of women in line with the needs of the secular Republic ultimately brought about the "replacement of Islamic patriarchy with Western patriarchy" whereby women's rights and freedoms, their role in public life as well as in the domestic sphere continued to be determined by men (Arat, 1998).

In any case, the Republic was successful in creating a population of educated and cultured women who considered family and work "sacred" which ultimately led to an extensive professional labor force as early as the first decades of twentieth century (Öncü, 1981; Balım-Harding, 1999, p. 112). Regarding women in the judiciary, for instance, judicial statistics on number of women judges have only started to be collected after 2006, but they demonstrate a slow yet somewhat steady increase in the last decade, from 28% in 2006 to 43% in 2018.[6] Feminization is also meaningful in the context of a steady increase in population as well as in the number of judges per 100,000 inhabitants from 8.9 in 1997 to 13.9 in 2017 (HSK, 2018a, p. 82). Meanwhile, the 2018 report by European Commission for the Efficiency of Justice (CEPEJ) based on 2016 data from 45 countries shows an overall average of 49% for male and 51% for women judges with a general trend toward an increase in the percentage of women. Hence parallel to the global trend, it is possible to say that the judiciary in Turkey has also been feminizing and given the increasing percentages of women at law faculties, this trend is likely to continue. Figure 1 shows the increase in the percentage of women judges since 2006.

Despite increasing percentages, there remains a gendered segregation that works to the disadvantage of women in the judiciary, as is the case in the rest of the world (CEPEJ, 2018). Horizontally, this segregation can be observed in the uneven distribution of women judges in different jurisdictions. While women judges constitute the majority of judges in family courts, they seem to be much less visible in superior criminal courts or in commercial courts. Women are also underrepresented in prosecution with 11% as of 2018 (HSK, 2018b). In terms of vertical segregation, women in the judiciary are also distributed unequally along the stages of professional development mainly due to an "ordering based on 'desirable' attributes – income, prestige, job stability, etc." (EGGE, 2009). In the Turkish judiciary, women seldom get to be Chief Prosecutors in charge of monitoring and controlling the work of prosecutors, while they only constitute 14% of Court presidents (CEPEJ, 2018, 117).

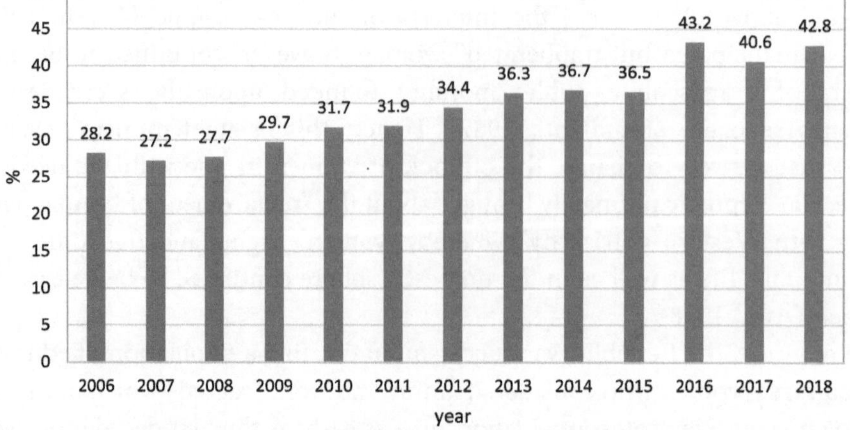

Figure 1. Percentage of women judges in Turkey (2006–2018) (HSK, 2018b).

3. Woman vs. Judge and what it takes to be both

In the period of December 2015–April 2016, I talked to seven women judges from different lower courts. Except for one in Ankara, all judges were from Istanbul courts. Table 1 shows the cities, the courts, the ages and years of experience of the interviewed judges.

From a feminist epistemological and methodological standpoint, I wanted to explore whether gender emerges as a meaningful category in the ways these judges reflect upon their professional journey. I did not ask them questions about being a woman from the outset. Instead, I wanted them to walk me through their life in general, starting with their families, upbringings and continuing with their decisions to become a judge. I refrained from asking direct questions on gender and how it has shaped their relations, but since they were informed about the objectives of the study, they would ultimately start talking about being a woman. They talked about being a girl in their family, a young woman in internship and early posts, a mother, a wife and a woman judge. It was not just about sharing difficulties or obstacles faced as a woman either; it was also about revealing their own ways of dealing with these. These women are powerful professionals who hold significant public authority in their hands, so they told stories of defying the male dominance in their families, of resisting male colleagues' attempts to question their competence, of developing strategies to manage institutional sexism and male judicial culture. But they are also women of humble backgrounds, born and raised in this patriarchal and conservative culture; so their narratives were also interwoven with stories of balancing work and family, of playing along lines of masculinity in order to be taken seriously and hiding their sexuality.

Judges talked about their professional journey in reference to two distinct stages: their training and their time on the bench. Next two sections will therefore follow this periodization.

3.1. Becoming a judge – the training

In Turkey, law is studied as a four-year undergraduate education modeled after continental European legal training. During their education, law students are not offered different tracks; so after they graduate, they have to decide whether they

Table 1. Information on interviewed judges.

	City	Jurisdiction	Age (2016)	Experience
Judge 1	Istanbul	Criminal Court	59	35 years
Judge 2	Istanbul	Criminal Court	52	29 years
Judge 3	Ankara	Labor Court	54	32 years
Judge 4	Istanbul	Court of Enforcement	46	21 years
Judge 5	Istanbul	Labor Court	58	29 years
Judge 6	Istanbul	Civil Court	58	33 years
Judge 7	Istanbul	Family	48	19 years

want to become a lawyer or apply for civil service as a judge or a prosecutor. Prospective lawyers continue with a one-year internship, at court and next to a practicing lawyer; while graduates who want to become a judge or a prosecutor have to take a written and an oral exam followed by a 17 month-long professional training.[7] After deciding on their track, candidates then draw lots to determine their first assignment as a judge or a prosecutor. Turkey is administratively divided into 81 provinces and these are judicially clustered in five districts according to economic conditions, the availability of health, social and cultural services, their proximity to city centers and other relevant geographical factors, etc. Typically, at the beginning of their careers, judges are appointed to fifth districts which are mostly rural provinces with relatively less workload. In small provinces, it is also not uncommon to have a single court that handles both civil and criminal cases, so judges also get to experience different types of adjudication and proceedings before they move to a higher district. In this system, by the time a judge reaches the first district, he/she would typically have about 15 years of experience on the bench.[8]

This system is also quite gendered. During the compulsory training, candidates are already strained by moral pressures as they are expected to live in a way that is appropriate for the profession. The example of Didem Yaylalı, a candidate judge who committed suicide, can be given as an example of this oppressive environment. Yaylalı faced a disciplinary proceeding for her failure to fully attend her internship which in fact she justified with a medical report. However, there was reportedly also a process of naming and shaming going on with rumors about her not being fit for the profession because "she was wearing skinny pants, drinking, hanging out at night" (Köksal, 2015). Her suicide was linked to this humiliating process at the end of which she was denied the right to practice her profession. This incident is also reflexive of a larger cultural context where social norms of conduct are much more limiting for women.[9]

At the same time, internship is also a specific period where judges and prosecutors get to meet each other socially and most probably even find their partners for marriage. This is significant because after the internship and exams, candidates are assigned to their initial posts in rural areas of the country. This assignment is already quite challenging for a young – they get their first posts around age 24–25 – and inexperienced judge, and it gets to be even more difficult for a woman. In the following excerpt, a woman judge is talking about how in the rural areas not only you need the help of men for manual tasks, but you are also under scrutiny for moral reasons. Here the judge talks about how a male colleague found it highly inappropriate when a woman prosecutor offered to sublet her own place to him when she was taking a leave of absence.

> Our working conditions are very tough. As a young and single woman, you cannot live in Yüksekova.[10] You need to have your fire set up, you ask for help. Many colleagues go

> to their initial posts with their parents. This profession is not for weak and single women. For example, a woman prosecutor friend of mine, was going on a leave, and a male prosecutor would temporarily replace her. My friend offered him her place because it was hard to find a place to stay there. The male prosecutor said to me 'can you believe this woman?!' (6)

So, judges usually try to choose their partners before their initial post so that they can benefit from what is called the "couples' lottery". All prospective judges and prosecutors draw a lot at the end of their training to determine their first assignment.[11] For married couples, there is a separate one that allows them to be assigned to the same province which is generally an urban one. One of the judges explained the reason for assigning married couples to more developed provinces in terms of conflict of interest which ultimately turns marriage into an advantage.

> Why couples' lottery? Couples cannot work in small places. A prosecutor cannot ask the judge to issue a pretrial detention if she is his wife! That is why couples can only work in jurisdictions with two or more judges. And those provinces are usually third regions with five or six judges. This also becomes a difficulty for the singles. Since we singles work in small provinces, our social circle is also very small. I have always worked in places with two judges and one prosecutor. But those friends always work in provinces with more couples, so their circle also expands. That is why judges marrying each other is a right and useful thing. (1)

Judges also prefer to be married before their initial post so that they will not be alone in remote parts of the country which is a fear that is triggered quite often during the internship. Women candidates are said to be particularly affected by rumors about the poor conditions in remote eastern provinces which push them into marriage. Interestingly, the same issue of going away alone has also been interpreted by another judge as a legitimate excuse for moving out of her family household. She specifically told a story of deciding to become a judge so that she could be free as a woman. She said that while she was doing her internship, an encounter with her parents made her realize that if she were to become a lawyer, she would not be able to leave her family and live on her own in a socially acceptable way. When her parents offered to set up an office for her and her brother who was also studying law, she realized that they would continue to have control over her life even if she was making an independent living. As a lawyer she had the freedom to choose where to practice and her family would push her to stay and work close to them. As a judge, however, she would have to go away for compulsory service in other parts of the country. Besides, even if she wanted to leave her family and live on her own, it would still not be acceptable in the 1980s Ankara.[12]

This yearning for freedom emerges in other narratives as well. Another judge explained how she in fact wanted to study outside Istanbul so that she could be free but had to go to Istanbul University Law Faculty when she could not get into any other. She even mentioned that although she studied in Ankara for a year, she was not free there either because her extended family forced her to live with them (6). This narrative was coupled with remarks on her enmity towards her patriarchal family where men were privileged.

> My strength grew out of the conflict in my family. Because my brother was always favored in the distinction between woman and man. The foundation of my power and success is this race with my brother. It was about showing the family that men in fact were nothing … I proved myself. My philosophy was always being on my own. Making money and moving out. Back then these were unthinkable for a Black Sea family.[13] I never dreamed of marriage. My philosophy was not being dependent on a father or a husband. (6)

The ways in which these women frame their reasons for becoming a judge reveal the embedded expectations, concerns and struggles associated with being a woman in Turkish society. Above all and most vividly, their search for freedom is entrenched within gendered social norms, expectations and traditions. Even when they talk about coming from somewhat educated, cultured, or at least rather supportive families, some of them still refer to their need to break free from their environments and to gain independence economically as well as socially.[14]

3.2. Being a judge – the bench

When women judges talk about the difficulties of the profession and their workload, they specifically refer to the sacrifices they have to make. When they see less of their children due to professional responsibilities, miss their school events, or cannot fulfill their household responsibilities or even when they fail to attend to their husbands' needs, women feel like these are necessary sacrifices if they want to be a judge. And they even have to give up more if they want to be better judges than men, a requirement for being taken seriously as a professional. This compulsory balance between their work and family life is the main yardstick against which their competence as a woman judge is measured. When they reflect upon their careers, they cite instances of less experienced men getting their positions, or of conservative inspectors implying that women judges belong to the household, or of unseen, informal yet very powerful barriers obstructing their professional advancement because they fail to socialize properly.[15]

3.2.1. Professional rigor and effects on family life: stories of 'sacrifice'

One apparent framework within which gender emerged as a seminal component of the professional experience was the rigor associated with the job. Women judges have all talked about how demanding the profession is. Indeed, with an average of 20–30 cases per day, these judges have quite a heavy caseload. Hence, long shifts, working over the weekends, taking case files home and lack of institutional support are usually cited as the most compelling features of this profession.[16] The underlining theme of "sacrifice" surrounds all narratives and is almost always explained in reference to the challenges of keeping a balance between work and family. Women judges talk about how having a successful career and raising kids at the same time is not possible and how they have prioritized their work over their families. These sacrifices become even more challenging in the context of insufficient institutional support like childcare arrangements, flexible working hours or parental leave. Even in the interview where the respondent felt she had a relatively easier experience with child rearing, she said it was because she had kids during her internship which she completed in a big city. She said that by the time she finished her internship and was assigned to her initial post as a judge, her kids were already big enough to go to some sort of childcare facility and she did not have to worry about leaving them at home with a babysitter in a place she was not familiar with (7).[17] In fact, she explained her whole child rearing experience as one of "good luck" because she always worked in big towns where she could actually have access to such facilities and the reason for that allocation was because she benefited from couples' lottery.

> I mean when you look at it logically it makes sense. Why? At the end of the day, he is your colleague, you have common interests, it will be to your advantage in the places you are appointed to. So, if you also have a mental agreement of some sort, there isn't really any reason for why you should not be married. (2)

This "instrumentality of the wife-husband relationship" (Kandiyoti, 1987, p. 326) also makes particular sense to women because when their husbands are also from the profession, compulsory relocations do not turn into a major distress for their family life and they can also seek compassion from their husbands when they neglect their family responsibilities because they have too much work to do. Men, however, are not always willing to provide support or understanding. In general, they even prefer to marry housewives or women from other typically gendered professions like teachers because they do not want their partners to neglect their families like women judges do. This is parallel to the existing social structure.[18]

> It is troubling even if your husband is from the profession. It is especially difficult for women judges when their husband is not their colleague. Rightfully, the man wants to invite people over, or he wants to go out. My husband would not bring cases home, but I would … But a different profession is too difficult. But not for male judges, they marry teachers. They want a partner who can organize housework, take care of the children. They marry colleagues as a second option. Women judges around me are all married to their colleagues. (7)

Nonetheless, even in marriages where both parties are judges, sacrifices are always seen as belonging to the woman. For example, one of my respondents told how her husband who is also a judge would react against her workload and tell her not to bring cases home.

> … I always prioritized my work. My husband would say enough, do not bring files back home. I would leave my child burning with fever and come to work. I would go to the field, come back home with my breast filled up with milk only to find that my husband fed the baby thinking that I was not coming home … But the woman has to keep this balance. Your husband says the child is sick what are you doing, and you say I have files to read and he says the hell with your files! (3)

In the absence of other institutional support mechanisms, this dependency on the "compassion" of the other partner becomes key for women judges (Mehdi, 2017, p. 231). Even in cases where the partner is described as supportive, the story is never one of complete equality in terms of division of labor in the household. One of the judges mentioned her husband's – who is not a judge – support for her professional as well as social work, but then added "But he did not make my life that easy. When I am away, he calls me in the morning to ask me where the children's socks are" (3). This dual role assumed by judges is an extension of a larger social reality of women working a "second shift" at home in Turkey (Hochschild, 1990; İlkkaracan, 1998) which is in fact in line with the original image of the Republican woman (Acar, 1998, p. 314; O'Neill and Güler, 2009).

Interestingly, however, these narratives also display a representation of marriage as a safeguard for women judges in terms of their professional life.[19]

Children, however, are a different story. One of the judges openly said that in Ankara, and particularly at the Court of Appeals, "they do not like women who give birth" (3). She talked about how especially male judges always have prejudices against women colleagues thinking that they always "go to tea parties, give birth and take maternity leave, lay their work upon men". In another interview, the respondent mentioned if she cannot go to work when her kid is sick and gets a medical record for her absence, she would at the very least get a sarcastic smile from her male colleagues (5). Interestingly, while men question the professional competence of women who give birth, at the same time they expect them to be less dedicated to their work and pay more attention to their families. In the following incident, the woman judge talked about how an inspector was jealous of her professionally and resorted to sexist comments in order to get rid of her.[20]

> There was once an extremely conservative inspector. The respect of the people on the street towards me affected him. He asked my husband whether I was planning to quit, that I should take care of my children at home …. (6)

Similarly, another judge mentioned a conservative male colleague who believed that she should cut her shift short and go home to her child instead.

> I come to the courthouse early in the morning and don't leave until the end of my regular working hours. There was a more conservative male colleague. There was the expectation that I should go home when my hearings are over, that I have a small child, I should take care of him, that I did not need to stay at the courthouse. (4)

There is of course an overt sexism in all such comments. Also, again in the absence of institutional support, judges' compulsory relocations make house and childcare much more dependent upon the changing conditions of the work sites (Mehdi, 2017, p. 226). In fact, they frequently mentioned how in rural parts, leaving their kids to young village girls would make them very nervous but they would not have a choice (5). But again, this was an issue that needed to be managed by these women without much fuss, and certainly without affecting their competence at work.

> I mean finding a woman to take care of my child is my responsibility. I should not talk about this at the courthouse, especially among my male colleagues. I mean I should not talk about my child's sickness with them. This is my problem and I am able to take care of it. It makes us show a special effort not to bring our personal problems, those stemming from motherhood, from being a wife, being a woman to our work environment. For example, you are pregnant, but you should exist in the courthouse environment without letting your nausea or difficulties be sensed by the outside. Why? Because a male colleague can think like "OK, she will take a leave in two months". (2)

All these narratives reveal the gendered structure of professional life with respect to institutional and socio-cultural expectations from women judges which they have internalized. Professional hardships are also the basis for culturally conservative attacks against these women. The next section will deal with how these challenges ironically create better judges because women feel like they have to be more careful, make less mistakes, and look more work oriented and detached in order to prove their professional competence.

3.2.2. Work harder, work more: challenges making "better judges"

Narratives on the hardships of the profession and the challenges faced while trying to balance work and family, are always accompanied with references to how women judges struggle to prove their competence as a judge against all these odds. The constant questioning of their professional capacity ultimately forces them to be more hard-working, more diligent and more successful at decision making. In fact, respondents consider women judges' professional competence and their dedication to their job as a problem for the predominantly male judiciary; not because they perform weak or weaker, as expected by male colleagues, but rather because they in fact perform well, if not better. This has been expressed by some respondents as a source of concern on behalf of their male colleagues.

> Even if we have the exact same qualifications, our chances of getting to top positions are 1/3 of men. The only reason is gender. It is the mentality. I guess men do not want to lose their domain. Women show more effort, work more in order to make up the gender disadvantage. This effort disturbs men. (5)

Another judge believed that men feel threatened by women in professional life because "they cannot accept the fact that women are meticulous, and that they are better than them" (2). So, men's suspicion towards professional women is in fact not concerned with women's capacity to deliver whatever the job requires; it is rather concerned with women being better at doing it. This is why women judges believe they are allowed only a very low margin of error because any small mistake they make will be seen as a problem for the work they do: "Hence it will not be just your mistake; it will be the mistake of the woman judge" (2). This sense of entitlement among male judges which makes them see themselves as "natural occupants of such positions" ultimately creates a work environment under "heightened attention", as Hunter – borrowing from Rosabeth Moss Kanter – calls it, which is an experience among women judges whereby their professional qualifications are under constant surveillance (2006, p. 295). Women's attention to detail and careful examination of files then becomes a strategy to prove that they are just as good as men on the bench.

However, professional pressures are not the only reason why women judges believe they are ultimately better in their work. They also referred to the enclosed nature of the profession in the sense of not socializing with the outside world (Balcı, 2018, p. 139). This is a common rhetoric in the judiciary where independence of the judges is understood in terms of not being in touch with society at large. Very often judges and prosecutors live quite secluded lives both professionally and personally where they only socialize with each other at work and at home. They live at public housing facilities reserved for the judicial staff, ride in the same shuttles to the courthouse, and go to same summer facilities. In one of the interviews, the respondent talked about this professional isolation as a socially incapacitating feature of being a judge. She complained about how this seclusion in fact trapped judges and prosecutors in their own circles, surrounding them with inquiring gazes of the people as well as the authorities.

> We are always like that. We graduate like that. They tell us you cannot talk to anybody except this and that. We are concerned about what we will do when we retire! You do not have anybody around you except judges and prosecutors. You have no social contacts. You cannot get together with people from outside. You should be able to as long as it is not abused. But you do not know really what the citizen will do especially in small places. We are always surrounded. (7)

This specific reference to the significance of keeping a certain "social distance" from the community especially in rural places was also observed by Junqueira in the Brazilian context (2003, p. 442). She argues that in these small provinces judges are required to keep this distance for an image of impartiality and authority; and the community also contributes to it by showing respect to the judges. This "reciprocal process of self-imposed and community imposed isolation" poses extra hardships for women judges not only because it constrains their behaviors with stricter social and cultural norms, "since the community is permanently watching their behaviors"; but also because it delimits their possibilities for emotional relationships (Junqueira, 2003, p. 443). Junqueira argues that although "suitable behavior is required from all judges because they are figures of authority", in small towns different moral expectations are in fact applied to men and women (2003, p. 443). Hence, when it comes to women judges, the required isolation of the profession cannot solely be understood in reference to impartiality; it also needs to be considered in the context of gendered cultural codes and values that supersede professional authority. In Turkey, professional seclusion also has a resonance of social conservatism that is maintained by typical gender roles and expectations. One of the women judges, for instance, argued that they are more "inaccessible" because "they are dedicated to their homes, they go to work and come back home in the afternoon" (1). This statement is not particularly about women working harder than men; rather, it implies how women are less distracted by external influences that could jeopardize their professional integrity (5). Hence, it implies a reference to different socialization opportunities between women and men in the judiciary which ultimately influence the kind of judge they turn out to be.[21] Respondents believe that the exclusion of women judges from beneficial socialization opportunities makes them less open to manipulation and hence more successful at protecting the profession: "They cannot approach women easily. Women protect the profession. It is easier to approach men. It is easier to detect their weaknesses and approach them" (5).[22]

Socialization, however, is also the primary key to step up in the professional ladder.[23] Women judges openly state that they are always less preferred for positions of authority because they have fewer opportunities to introduce themselves to the selection committees which are predominantly male (1). Male judges are always depicted as being more successful at lobbying because they can easily arrange "Ankara visits" where they get to introduce themselves to selection committees for possible promotions or establish contacts and promote themselves over social events like dinners or drinks or even religious practices like Friday prayers. All these occasions are predominantly women free. Exclusion from these networking opportunities also result with women being denied access to significant flows of information that can in fact change one's professional course of events. Junqueira, for instance, talks about how women lawyers in Brazil find it more difficult to engage in beneficial networking activities because of their family responsibilities which creates different specialization areas for women and men (2003, p. 441). Ultimately, although women judges seem to believe they are better at judging because of the extra effort they put in and their relative seclusion from external pressures, when it comes to getting to the top of judicial hierarchy, they remain way behind.

> The fact that the profession is a closed one, that the social circle is not wide made women more successful. They did not receive directives from anybody, they have been more successful. They are better judges in terms of decisions. But this success did not have a consequence. How many women judges preside at Commercial

> Courts or how many women judges sit at the Court of Appeals? They are in fact better professionally. (6)

These narratives once again demonstrate how professional life is always molded within the larger social norms and cultural expectations. This becomes even more apparent in the ways in which women judges strategize to be accepted as equal professionals in the judiciary.

3.2.3. Male judicial culture

Narratives on the difficulties of balancing personal life and work, on the sacrifices women judges must make, on their obligation to work more than men in order to prove their professional competence, on their common exclusion from beneficial social gatherings, all reflect the highly masculine character of the judiciary. Liberal law reflects the values, the priorities and experiences of men; and mostly white, elite, urban men. Hence, it is no wonder that the judiciary is also male and that the "default judge" who is perceived to be impartial and dehumanized is in fact a man (Rackley, 2013). These qualities shape the ways in which we imagine the legal world and especially decision making to such an extent that when a woman sits on the bench, her professional performance is always measured against a backdrop of her "feminine qualities" that can possibly impair her judgment. Women judges in Turkey also talk about how they are always addressed as "Hakim Bey", especially at the beginning of their career.[24] One of the judges explained how this expression was in fact an indication of the suspicion towards her capacity as a judge.

> Mr. Judge is the usual expression. Even if you are a woman, they continue to call you Mr. Judge … It is like you feel the suspicion that you will not be able to succeed. But if they can feel that power in your attitude, or if they see you on top of the tractor on the field, then they think oh there is no difference. (4)

Particularly in rural provinces women judges are seen as "temporarily occupying the seats that in fact belong to male judges", as "sitting in their place" (1). One of the judges explained how in one of these provinces where she worked as a criminal judge, her presence was denied to such an extent that local officers would in fact push the prosecutor – who was her husband – to exert professional control over her.

> The police were not used to seeing a woman judge. They would complain about me to Mr. Prosecutor. So would the chief clerk at the court. And the prosecutor was my husband! I mean not like an official complaint, but rather like a reproach. They tried to monitor me with my husband. They would say, "Mrs. Judge is not arresting, can you say something?" My husband and I had a deal. He would also send me files that could not go to arrest so that it would not look like the prosecutor sends and the judge arrests. (6)

These narratives are ultimately related to a common image of the profession as being powerful and authoritarian, qualities that are both associated with masculinity. When women judges assume this authority, not only do they face a challenge in terms of the public's recognition of it, but they also feel like they have to prove to their male colleagues that they are not different from them. Hence, the dominant masculine culture requires women judges to act like a man or at least to try not to look like an outsider in male conversations which include being informed about traditional male topics like football or cars. In such instances, given that male judges see them "first a woman, then a judge", women judges strive to embrace traditional male talk and masculine conduct in order to pass as "one of them" (Rackley, 2013). One of the judges, for instance, cited an incident where she wanted to join her male colleagues when they were invited by the District Governor to an evening out.

> The District Governor calls everyone and for instance they go to a belly dancing venue. I put a lot of fight for this! I said I will come too! If you are going as prosecutors and judges, I will come too. At the end, one of them said "Mrs. Judge" is one of us. That is how I could join them. (6)

In another instance, the same judge talked about how she does not allow her male colleagues to light her cigarette and even lights theirs which is seen as an act that does not really fit with generally accepted rules of social conduct between men and women. So, through these carefully chosen and strategic performances, women judges try to strip off their femininity in order to be taken seriously as a judge.

> You have to give the "I am not a woman, I am doing my job, I am a judge" message. The moment your femininity comes to the fore, you think they will not consider you a judge … you do not want that to shine. I did not want it as a woman. Why? Because the moment they are interested in your beauty, womanhood, motherhood, your identity as a judge will remain in the background. (2)

In this professional setting, women judges not only strive to demonstrate that they are equally "good judges" by proving that they can be rational, that they do not decide with emotions, that they are impartial (Kenney, 2013, p. 144); but they also feel the burden to present themselves as asexual in order to be taken seriously as a professional. Schultz and Shaw, borrowing from Junqueira, argue that "the robe that attracts respect from the outside world helps women to adapt to the ruling image thereby turning themselves into 'asexual beings'" (2013a, p. 25; Junqueira, 2003, p. 446). This has a lot to do with the existing cultural suppression of female sexuality in Turkey. Gendered attitudes towards sexuality become most manifest in the pervasive image of women's sexuality as a threat to public morality that needs to be controlled by the patriarchal society. Only recently, in 2005, with the amendments to the Penal Code, crimes against female sexuality were no longer defined as crimes against public morality.

This becomes very clear in the relative disadvantage that single women face in networking opportunities. All respondents believe that it is harder for women judges to leave their families, children, pass their domestic responsibilities, etc. in order to join certain networking events. However, this type of socialization is still harder for single or divorced women because their presence at such events would raise even more controversies within the judicial setting, leading to gossips, improper comments, jokes, etc. (1) One of the married judges talked about how being married was a "shield" that protected women from improper gestures or comments at such events. She then shared an incident when she stood up for a single woman judge who was in fact being harassed by fellow male judges. This piece of information was particularly valuable because it was reflexive of those rare moments of solidarity between women judges against the blatant cultural sexism that made institutional discrimination invisible.

> Once, on the shuttle, I witnessed a male judge openly making a pass at a woman judge at least ten years younger than him. Other men were also trailing. But the woman was uncomfortable, trying to ignore it. I could not take it anymore and said, "enough, it is no longer a joke!" When you are married, they cannot do this. (6)

This was in line with a single woman judge's comment on how, as in other areas of social life, women in the judiciary were also under pressure to act in certain ways and how she has to turn down dinner invitations because she is concerned about reactions that can harm her professional life (1). Such self-censorship mechanisms regulating the boundaries of socially – not professionally – acceptable behavior are quite common among women judges. One of the judges talked about how she tried to normalize the incident of "a man entering her chamber" for her court staff. She talked about how the moment a strange man enters her room, either someone from the clerk office or a male colleague would inquire about the identity of the guest asking if he is her brother or cousin and how she would always speak the truth in order to break these prejudices. Women judges quite often referred to these "appropriate" modes of entering each other's chambers and gave examples of how these depended on gender as well as marital status of the judge.

> Women judges do not like other women judges entering their husbands' chambers. This is even more drastic for single women judges because they are scared of gossip … You pay more attention to this in the rural areas. You do not go to a male judge's chamber.

Yet another respondent claimed that being divorced was in fact even worse than being single since after her divorce she was always seen as a "potential threat" by men and by other women judges alike (2). Once again, marriage turned out to be an advantage for women in the judicial world. When it comes to famous Ankara visits, for instance, married women were described as having more possibilities for promoting themselves since they can go to Ankara with their husbands.[25] In the following quote, a single woman judge talks about how it is easier for married women judges to engage in networking because they attend such activities with their partners.

> They go together; they can more easily introduce themselves to those people who will do the selection. They go out to dinner together, they socialize. We are more timid about this matter. Is this because of us? No ... It is because of the ways in which those male friends look at us. (1)

In all these narratives, men are seen as making women feel like they are always in a race with them which is not a professional race but rather a "race with gender" (2). This race is partly managed throughout the professional journey as women judges learn to perform in ways that allow them access into the male world; and it seems to come to an end as they get older and hence are no longer seen as "sexual objects" (6). The moment that a woman judge is no longer seen feminine, she no longer constitutes a reason for male colleagues to constrain their subjects of converse or control their language in her presence. Women judges feel like they can set themselves free from these pressures to act like men or to protect themselves from them when they no longer pose a sexual threat for this masculine community.

> I guess it happened when I no longer had a problem with getting married. It was the moment when I said I can now talk comfortably with everyone, they will not think of me in those terms, they will not think that I have a weakness for them. (1)

4. Discussion

This study intended to look into how gender plays out in the professional and social performances of women judges in Turkey. Women in the judiciary, as in other professions, have been facing obstacles all around the world (Schultz and Shaw, 2013b, 2014; Sonneveld and Lindbekk, 2017). As a social process, however, gender also needs to be contextualized through empirical observation (Kandiyoti, 1987). Beyond commonalities in experiences of women professionals around the world, stories of woman judges also need to be considered against a backdrop of larger historical, social and cultural processes. In this study, therefore, I introduced the Republican regime as the structural and ideological framework within which women's role in public life needs to be understood in Turkey; and I tried to situate the narratives of women judges within the predicament of Turkey's modernization and its take on women.

Sancar argues that with all the reforms and improvements regarding the role of women in this society, Turkish modernization is one where "men make the State and women make the family" (Sancar, 2012). In this model of late modernization, one that is founded upon a combination of conservatism and nationalism, men contribute to women's participation in public sphere by offering them education, but they never actually consider them their equals. Hence despite significant legal developments that granted women unprecedented rights as early as the 1920s, many elements of the traditional gender relations, particularly concerning the role of women in marriage and family were kept intact. Women of the new Republic were equipped with "education and finer skills, only to improve their contribution to the Republican patriarchy as better wives and mothers" which would prove the resoluteness of this new nation (Arat, 1998, p. 52).

At the same time, these women were also expected to be virtuous, honorable and committed citizens who were stripped off their sexuality in public life. Hence, they continued to carry the burden of patriarchal moral codes and gendered expectations of appropriate social conduct. In her nominal essay on the relation between Islam and the status of women in Republican Turkey, Toprak asks whether women's emancipation has in fact brought their liberation (1982). Her argument regarding the prevalence of the role of Islam in women's continuing subordination to male authority in modern Turkey was later developed by Kandiyoti who argued that the State in fact plays a crucial role in determining the role and impact of religion in the lives of women; and in that sense the new Republic had a "progressive impact on women's rights", but it has also contributed to the maintenance of existing controls of female sexuality (Kandiyoti, 1987). In 1990, Toprak further argued that emancipation was a legal issue which has been effective in Turkey, but that liberation also involved being free of the pressures of cultural traditions and social expectations which has not been the case for women in Turkey, not even for the educated ones (1990). After all, the "secular daughter of the Republic" was a woman who

> had to be educated to Western standards but would be aware of her traditions and culture; she would be both free in mixing with males but also careful about her virtues, and she would have a strong sense of morals. She was expected to suppress her sexuality and individuality, be serious, unassuming, compassionate and motherly. (Balım-Harding, 1999, p. 109)

Hence, for women in Turkey "sexual promiscuity remained to be a taboo" and female sexuality continued to be under the protection of family in rural and urban communities alike (Toprak, 1990, p. 42). There is in fact ample evidence that proves that the "ideal woman" in Turkey is still one who "is equal to men, works and makes money when needed, but does not suspend her roles as a mother and a wife in the family and even quits work if it hinders her household responsibilities, and does not hurt her husband's dignity by acting against codes of honor" (Yılmaz, 2012). 2006 and 2012 nationwide surveys showed that family – and woman's role and sexuality as an integral part of it – is still the cornerstone of conservatism in Turkish society (Yılmaz, 2012). In fact, participants of both surveys cited family as the most important social institution that needs to be preserved before religion, nation and state and women were considered as the main components of this domestic sphere.[26]

Concerning women judges, their experiences as described here also bring out social conservatism as the main modus operandi of gendered hierarchies in the judicial environment. When they are asked to reflect upon what it means to be a woman in Turkish judicial culture, judges' narratives reveal that starting with their training and early posts, gender emerges and continues to be a defining feature of their professional journey. Even the decision to become a judge, rather than a lawyer or a prosecutor, can be framed in reference to implications of gender in their lives. These implications can be felt either professionally or personally. When they are discouraged to pursue a career in prosecution because it is not competent with other social roles assigned to women, they are inclined to make other professional choices. Or when they in fact want to become a lawyer, their desire to set themselves free from their families and from the pressures of their communities pushes them towards civil service. Even their most personal decisions, like when and who they will marry, are in fact influenced by these gendered realities, not only of the profession but of the society at large. Hence, a young woman judge who is set out to practice her profession at a remote part of the country has to consider how she will survive on her own if she is not married. Hence, while on the one hand a young woman law graduate can decide to become a judge to free herself from social pressures, she can end up confining herself within the boundaries of another constraining familial setting.

In these narratives, professional difficulties on the bench are never explained simply as matters of hard work or institutional deficiencies either. Women judges always remember these hardships in reference to the cultural and social meaning of being a woman in this society. When they talk about the balance between their work and family life and how they are always expected to choose the latter when in conflict, they are not only referring to a lack of institutional support. They also frame their experiences in reference to overarching cultural expectations from women in this highly patriarchal social order. Similarly, their stories on not having access to beneficial social networks or how they would have to look asexual in order not to be seen as a threat or to avoid rumors all intertwine with implicit notions of honour commonly defined over female sexuality.

Granted, women in Turkey were appointed to the bench quite early compared to their colleagues in many developed countries like France (1946), UK (1945) or Denmark (1933). Their situation also followed a significantly different trajectory than their counterparts in other Muslim majority countries where women's entry into the legal field was not only quite late but also seriously resisted (Cardinal, 2017; Lindbekk, 2017). On the other hand, Republican elites' support for women's entry into professional world remained mainly ideological and instrumental; creating a serious momentum in the status of women in the Turkish society, but not aiming for complete gender equality in legal, political spheres or in everyday life (Arat, 2000). These narratives of women judges demonstrate that the status of women in contemporary Turkey is still largely shaped in reference to cultural codes and expectations that reflect the patriarchal and conservative foundation of the society. The limits of women's individuality and femininity are still measured against the interests of the family and the community, and female sexuality remains subordinated to male honour and its control by public morality. It is in this sense that these judges also represent the modernist dilemma of the Republic. While on the one hand they represent the secular, emancipatory face of the regime with their education, financial freedom and respectable profession that grants them serious public authority; on the other hand, they are still expected to prioritize family over work, to behave in the appropriate fashion determined by men and to hide their femininity in order to be taken seriously.

These narratives, however, are also testimonies to the significance of having women judges on the bench as they also reveal struggles, strategies, victories of these women against the male judicial culture. Arzu Özpınar, a woman judge who was expelled from the profession because of allegedly unethical conduct like wearing too much make up, short skirts and having an affair with a married lawyer, resisted the decision and took her case to the ECHRts where the Court found her dismissal based on reasons relating to her private life in breach of the Convention (Kuyucu, 2015). Judge Didem Yaylalı, however, ended up taking her life because she could not stand similar allegations. What follows are how another woman judge expressed Yaylalı's suffering and what it means to be a woman judge in Turkish judiciary.

> …
>
> Didem was naive, inexperienced. She has not yet witnessed the experiences of women judges and prosecutors. But being a woman judge meant;
>
> being investigated for her hair color or the length of her skirt,
>
> if she is single, having her private life being spied,
>
> if she is a mother, being subject to talk on how she neglects her work because of her child (in reality women judges usually do not witness their kids growing up),
>
> not running for positions that the masculine judicial authority so generously distributes among male judges and prosecutors like head prosecution, court presidency or commission presidency,
>
> if she is applying for an investigative judge position at the Court of Appeals, facing questions like "do you have kids?", "do you plan to get pregnant?", your motherhood being belittled with all these questions posed like you have committed or about to commit a crime,
>
> even when your partner is a judge, having a life where your work is always considered less important,

not being able to make decisions about your own life when you deliver the most fateful decisions about other people's,

accepting the secondary role given to women by patriarchal societies,

in short besides the heavy work load, having a heavy load of womanhood. (Köksal, 2015, p. 24)

Notes

1. For some exceptions, see (Kalem Berk, 2013; Kuyucu, 2015; Balcı, 2018).
2. Balcı talks about a similar experience with women legal professionals. When she was doing her research on women in different fields of legal practice, she also failed to reach her intended numbers. She interprets this reluctance also as a consequence of the failed coup upon these professionals (Balcı, 2018, p. 106).
3. As a peculiar understanding of secularism, Turkish laicism allows for a convenient instrumentalization of religion by the state. Reminiscent of the French laicité de combat, the principle allows for state control over religious institutions, practices and symbols in the public sphere.
4. Standard first instance courts with jurisdiction over small claims.
5. Kemalism is a term identified with the principles of Mustafa Kemal Atatürk and as such is used to denote the main ideology of the new Republic.
6. This is the total number including all the judges working in judicial proceedings, administrative proceedings, higher courts etc.
7. This period was reduced to one year after the high number of dismissals from the judiciary in the aftermath of the 2016 coup attempt. In order to fill in the vacant positions as fast as possible, the training and appointment process was accelerated for prospective judges and prosecutors.
8. As of 2018, there are 60 first districts in the judicial organization which are mostly city centers. Istanbul, the largest city with an approximate population of 16 million, holds twenty of these districts.
9. Junqueira makes a similar assessment for Brasil (2003).
10. A Kurdish district in southeastern Turkey.
11. An exemption here was 2006 appointments mentioned above.
12. Durakbaşa argues that:

    In 1990s Turkey women were still stigmatized for out of wedlock relations, they still faced difficulties when they try to rent a place on their own. They still needed their husbands' permission for abortion, were still victims of honour crimes, still had to leave their work when they marry. (1998, p. 31)

13. Referring to the conservative family and social structure of northern Turkey.
14. Regarding economic freedom, some women also mentioned how they never wanted to become lawyers because of financial challenges. One of them said she never liked advocacy because she witnessed lawyers not being paid or losing all their clients when they have a health issue, while another expressed her distaste for collecting fees from clients like a merchant. These reasonings ultimately point out to a certain need for financial security that is guaranteed by public service which is also a manifestation of the middle class and predominantly rural background of the judicial staff in Turkey (Cirhinlioğlu, 1997; Sancar and Ümit-Atılgan, 2009; Balcı, 2018, p. 128–129). Junqueira refers to the same phenomenon in Brazil where young people prefer public legal professions due to

financial security which is particularly crucial for women as it guarantees "peace of mind" (2003, p. 441).

15. Similar observations have been made about women lawyers in the UK (Sommerlad *et al.*, 2010; Rackley, 2013).
16. A similar observation was made by Junqueira for Brazilian judges more than a decade ago. Brazilian judges also primarily complained about the amount of work they have to undertake which requires their complete dedication (Junqueira, 2003, p. 443).
17. Tremblay refers to a similar line of thinking among women lawyers in Quebec who choose to have children very early, even before they begin their professional life. Hence, by the time they are in their 30s, their kids are older and these women feel like they can invest much more in their professional life (Tremblay, 2013, p. 13).
18. A 2018 survey on public's perceptions of gender reveals that 51% of men and 45% of women in Turkey believe that the primary duty of women is taking care of her household. The majority of people in Turkey are not against women working after marriage or giving birth ; nonetheless they are still more inclined to view domestic responsibilites as belonging to women (Kadir Has Üniversitesi Toplumsal Cinsiyet ve Kadın Çalışmaları Araştırma Merkezi, 2018).
19. A similar finding was found to be true for women in top executive positions in Turkey (Kabasakal, 1998, p. 312). For most women in Turkey, however, the effect of marriage on work is in fact quite different. Research showed that marriage exerts a serious pressure upon the lives of women in Turkey (İlkkaracan, 1998) with many women giving up work when they get married. On the other hand, the fact that work for many women is usually low paid, low skilled, insecure, with little opportunity for advancement, is also given as a possible reason for leaving it when they marry (O'Neill and Güler, 2009).
20. Constitutionally inspectors of the Ministry of Justice are responsible for auditing and investigating the work of judges and prosecutors for their professional and ethical performances. Inspectors are selected from among judges or prosecutors with credible records.
21. Like other women in the society, judges also benefit from each other or from their family members in terms of organizing child care (Kandiyoti, 1987, p. 330). Except for this cooperation, however, there is not much reference to alternative socialization activities among women judges nor is there much reference to solidarity between them aside from occasional anectodes on the positive influence of seeing older women on the bench.
22. Mehdi refers to a similar situation in Pakistan where "approachability" is in fact associated with "partiality, bribes, and other types of corruption". She then talks about how women judges' lack of approachability – due to social rules limiting their networking opportunities – simultaneously constrains their chances of engaging in corruption (Mehdi, 2017, p. 221–222).
23. The same reality applies to women lawyers in the form of "client development activities" (Tremblay, 2013, p. 19) or "rainmaking" (Junqueira, 2003, p. 441).
24. The Turkish term for a male judge.
25. As the capital city, situated in the very middle of the country, Ankara represents the power of the highly centralized state administration in Turkey. These visits to Ankara, therefore, imply critical bureaucratic encounters with influential people at the "center".
26. 41% of respondents in 2006 and 50% in the 2012 follow up agreed with this statement.

Disclosure statement

No potential conflict of interest was reported by the author.

ORCID

Seda Kalem http://orcid.org/0000-0002-2404-9429

References

Acar, F. (1998) Türkiye üniversitelerinde kadın öğretim üyeleri, in: A. Berktay-Hacımirzaoğlu (Ed) *75 yılda kadınlar ve erkekler. Bilanço 98 yazı dizisi* (İstanbul, Tarih Vakfı Yayınları), pp. 313–321.

Akyüz, H. *et al.* (2014) *Adaletin cinsiyeti: Erkek şiddeti ile mücadelede hukuki deneyimler* (İstanbul, Mor Çatı Yayınları).

Arat, Y. (1989) *Patriarchal Paradox: Women Politicians in Turkey.* London: Associated University Press.

Arat Y. (2000) From emancipation to liberation: the changing role of women in Turkey's public realm, *Journal of International Affairs*, 54(1), pp. 107–123.

Arat, Z. F. (1998) Kemalizm ve Türk kadını, in: A. Berktay-Hacımirzaoğlu (Ed) *75 yılda kadınlar ve erkekler. Bilanço 98 yazı dizisi* (İstanbul, Tarih Vakfı Yayınları), pp. 51–70.

Balcı, E. (2018) *Hukuk mesleklerinde kadınlar* (Ankara, Yetkin Yayınları).

Balım-Harding, Ç. (1999) Representations of Turkish women: objects of social engineering projects or individuals?, in: G. Jantzen (Ed) *Representations and Gender* (Manchester, John Rylands Library Publications), pp. 107–127.

Bülbül, D. (2015) Bir kadın yargıcın not defterinden, *Ankara Barosu Dergisi*, 73(4), pp. 303–306.

Cardinal, M. C. (2017) The politics of exclusion: women public prosecutors and criminal court judges in Syria (1975-2009), in: N. Sonneveld and M. Lindbekk (Eds) *Women Judges in the Muslim World: A Comparative Study of Discourse and Practice* (Leiden, Brill), pp. 237–258.

Cindoğlu, D. and Ünal, D. (2017) Gender and sexuality in the authoritarian discursive strategies of 'New Turkey', *European Journal of Women's Studies*, 24(1), pp. 39–54.

Cirhinlioğlu, Z., (1997) *Türkiye'de hukuk mesleği: Sosyolojik bir inceleme* (Ankara, Gündoğan Yayınları).

Durakbaşa, A. (1998) Cumhuriyet döneminde modern kadın ve erkek kimliklerinin oluşumu: Kemalist kadın kimliği ve 'münevver erkekler', in: A. Berktay-Hacımirzaoğlu (Ed) *75 yılda kadınlar ve erkekler. Bilanço 98 yazı dizisi* (İstanbul, Tarih Vakfı Yayınları), pp. 29–50.

European Commission for the Efficiency of Justice (CEPEJ). (2018) *European Judicial Systems Efficiency and Quality of Justice, CEPEJ Studies No: 6.*

European Commission's Expert Group on Gender and Employment (EGGE). (2009) *Gender Segregation in the Labour Market: Root Causes, Implications and Policy Responses in the EU.* Luxembourg: Publications Office of the European Union

Güneş-Ayata, A. (1998) Laiklik, güç ve katılım üçgeninde Türkiye'de kadın ve siyaset, in: A. Berktay-Hacımirzaoğlu (Ed) *75 yılda kadınlar ve erkekler. Bilanço 98 yazı dizisi* (İstanbul, Tarih Vakfı Yayınları), pp. 237–248.

Güneş-Ayata, A. and Doğangün, G. (2017) Gender politics of the AKP: restoration of a religio-conservative gender climate, *Journal of Balkan and Near Eastern Studies*, 19(6), pp. 610–627.

Hakimler Savcılar Kurulu (HSK). (2018a) *2017 yılı faaliyet raporu.* https://www.hsk.gov.tr/Eklentiler/files/HSK%202017%20YILI%20FAAL%C4%B0YET%20RAPORU.pdf

Hakimler Savcılar Kurulu (HSK). (2018b) *Hakimler ve Savcılar Kurulu istatistikleri.* http://www.hsk.gov.tr/Eklentiler/Dosyalar/5d7f48c3-7f89-4c3d-afc2-03923e3db661.pdf

Hochschild, A. (1990) *The Second Shift* (New York, Avon Books).

Hunter, R. (2006) The high price of success: the backlash against women judges, in: E. Sheehy and S. McIntrye (Eds) *Calling for Change: Women, Law, and the Legal Profession Ten Years After Touchstones for Change* (Ottawa, University of Ottowa Press), pp. 281–301.

İlkkaracan, İ. (1998) Kentli kadınlar ve çalışma yaşamı, in: A. Berktay-Hacımirzaoğlu (Ed) *75 yılda kadınlar ve erkekler.* Bilanço 98 yazı dizisi (İstanbul, Tarih Vakfı Yayınları), pp. 285–302.

Junqueira, E. B. (2003) Women in the judiciary: A perspective from Brazil, in: U. Schultz and G. Shaw (Eds) *Women in the World's Legal Professions* (London, Hart Publishing), pp. 437–450.

Kabasakal, H. (1998) Türkiye'de üst düzey kadın yöneticilerin profile, in: A. Berktay-Hacımirzaoğlu (Ed) *75 yılda kadınlar ve erkekler. Bilanço 98 yazı dizisi* (İstanbul, Tarih Vakfı Yayınları), pp. 303–312.

Kadir Has Üniversitesi Toplumsal Cinsiyet ve Kadın Çalışmaları Araştırma Merkezi. (2018) Türkiye'de toplumsal cinsiyet ve kadın algısı araştırması 2018.

Kalem Berk, S. (2013) Toplumsal cinsiyet ve profesyonelleşme: Hukuk mesleğinde kadın örneği, *Sosyoloji Araştırmaları Dergisi,* 16(1), pp. 75–103.

Kandiyoti, D. A. (1987) Emancipated but unliberated? Reflections on the Turkish case, *Feminist Studies,* 13(2), pp. 317–338.

Kenney, S. J. (2013) *Gender & Justice: Why Women in the Judiciary Really Matter* (New York and London, Routledge).

Köksal, L. (2015) Didem Yaylalı neden öldü?, *Ankara Barosu Dergisi,* 73(4), pp. 21–26.

Kuyucu, N. (2015) Muhafazakarlığın hedefinde bir kadın yargıç: AİHM'nin Özpınar kararı, *Ankara Barosu Dergisi,* 73(4), pp. 295–301.

Lindbekk, M. (2017) Women judges in Egypt: discourse and practice, in: N. Sonneveld and M. Lindbekk (Eds) *Women Judges in the Muslim World: A Comparative Study of Discourse and Practice* (Leiden, Brill), pp. 284–316.

Mehdi, R. (2017) Lady judges of Pakistan: embodying the changing living tradition of Islam, in: N. Sonneveld and M. Lindbekk (Eds) *Women Judges in the Muslim World: A Comparative Study of Discourse and Practice* (Leiden, Brill), pp. 204–236.

O'Neill, M. L. and Güler, F. (2009) The not so new Turkish woman: a statistical look at women in two Istanbul neighborhoods, *Journal of International Women's Studies,* 11(2), pp. 157–174.

Öncü, A. (1981) Turkish women in the professions: why so many?, in: N. Abadan Unat (Ed) (in collaboration with D. Kandiyoti and M. Kıray) *Women in Turkish Society* (Leiden, Brill), pp. 181–193.

Rackley, E. (2013) *Women, Judging and the Judiciary: From Difference to Diversity* (New York, Taylor and Francis).

Sancar, M. and Ümit-Atılgan, E. (2009) *"Adalet biraz es geçiliyor…" Demokratikleşme sürecinde hakimler ve savcılar* (İstanbul, TESEV Yayınları).

Sancar, S. (2012) *Türk modernleşmesinin cinsiyeti: Erkekler devlet, kadınlar aile kurar* (İstanbul, İletişim Yayınları).

Schultz, U. and Shaw, G. (2013a) Introduction: gender and judging: overview and synthesis, in: Schultz, U. and Shaw, G. (Eds) *Gender and Judging* (Oxford, Hart Publishing), pp. 3–47.

Schultz, U. and Shaw, G. (Eds) (2013b) *Gender and Judging.* Oxford: Hart Publishing.

Schultz, U. and Shaw, G. (Eds) (2014) *Women in the Judiciary* (New York, Routledge).

Sommerlad, H. *et al.* (2010) *Diversity in the Legal Profession in England and Wales: A Qualitative Study of Barriers and Individual Choice* (London, University of Westminster).

Sonneveld, N. and Lindbekk, M. (Eds) (2017) *Women Judges in the Muslim World: A Comparative Study of Discourse and Practice* (Leiden, Brill).

Tekeli, Ş. (1982) *Kadınlar ve siyasal toplumsal hayat* (İstanbul, Birikim).

Tepe, F. F. (2018) 2000'lerde türkiye'de kadın akademisyenler: Rol çatışması mı veya rol genişlemesi mi? *Yükseköğretim ve Bilim Dergisi/Journal of Higher Education and Science*, 8(2), pp. 271–279.

Toprak, B. (1982) Türk kadını ve din, in: N. Abadan Unat (Ed) *Türk toplumunda kadın* (İstanbul, Ekin Yayınları), pp. 361–374.

Toprak, B. (1990) Emancipated but unliberated women in Turkey: the impact of Islam, in: F. Özbay (Ed) *Women, Family and Social Change in Turkey* (Bangkok, UNESCO), pp. 39–49.

Tremblay, D. G. (2013) *Work-family balance for women lawyers today: a reality or still a dream?* Research note of the Community-University Research Alliance on work-life articulation over the lifecourse (CURA-WAROL) No 2013-9A.

Ülgen, C. and Ongun, C. (Eds) (2010) *Hukukun öncü kadını Avukat Süreyya Ağaoğlu* (İstanbul, İstanbul Barosu Yayınları).

Uygur, G. and Özdemir, N. (Eds) (2018) *Hukuk ve toplumsal cinsiyet çalışmaları* (Ankara, Seçkin Yayıncılık).

White, J. (2003) State feminism, modernization, and the Turkish Republican woman, *NWSA Journal*, 15(3), pp. 145–159.

Yılmaz, H. (2012) *Türkiye'de muhafazakarlık: Aile, cinsellik, din* (İki kamuoyu araştırmasının karşılaştırmalı bulguları, 2006 ve 2012).

A five-year gender equality score card for the Philippine Supreme Court under its first woman Chief Justice: opportunities seized and missed

Emily Sanchez Salcedo

ABSTRACT

On 24 August 2012, the Honourable Maria Lourdes Sereno was appointed Chief Justice of the Philippine Supreme Court, the first woman to hold such position since its establishment in 1901. Several cases involving important women's issues decided during her term were reviewed in this work, inspired by the possibility that a young, brilliant and hardworking woman of humble beginnings sitting at the helm could make a difference. Indeed, the Chief Justice manifested commendable grit in registering meaningful dissent in Imbong v. Ochoa, where she championed women's bodily autonomy, and when she wrote a provocative concurrence in Vinuya v. Romulo, where she gave hope to women who suffered wartime atrocities. However, she missed an opportunity to put the rape shield law into good use in deciding People v. Batuhan and Lacturan. Her concurrence was also disappointing in Garcia v. Drilon, where she favoured rational basis review over intermediate level of scrutiny for gender-based classification, in People v. Jumawan where a conviction for marital rape was based on romantic paternalism, in People v. Palotes where additional compensatory damages were not considered for a rape victim who bore a child, in People v. Tionloc where acquittal was based on rape myths, and in People v. Caoili where the Court refused to call rape by its ugly name.

Introduction

The highest court in the Philippine judicial system is the Supreme Court composed of a Chief Justice and 14 Associate Justices appointed by the President upon nomination by the Judicial and Bar Council.[1] On 24 August 2012, President Benigno Aquino III appointed Maria Lourdes Aranal Sereno (Sereno) as the 24th Chief Justice of the Philippine Supreme Court, the first woman to hold such position.

Sereno's appointment came at a time when two other women were also on the Supreme Court – Associate Justices Teresita Leonardo De Castro (De Castro) and Estela Perlas Bernabe (Bernabe). Out of 171 Justices appointed to the Supreme Court since its establishment on 11 June 1901, only 14 were women.

While three women constituted a minority in the 15-member Supreme Court, such number bears significance because most cases are decided in divisions of five members where the convergence of women's voices may be enough to make a difference. Moreover, for an institution overwhelmingly dominated by men for over a century, having a woman at the helm for the first time inspired visions of substantive change. As the Philippine Commission on Women had put it, Sereno's "expertise in gender analysis[2] and commitment to transparency will make way for reforms that make justice attuned to women's needs, particularly those who are from the poor and marginalized communities".[3]

Rosemary Hunter summarised current literature that support judicial diversity into six basic arguments as to why and how women can make a difference in judicial decision making. She characterised the first three arguments as symbolic, the fourth and fifth as practical, and the sixth as substantive.[4]

First, more women on the bench makes it more representative of the wider society and increases the democratic legitimacy of the judiciary. Second, the presence of women judges signals equality of opportunity for women in the legal profession. Third, the presence of women judges provide encouragement for more women to aspire for, seek and obtain judicial office which, in turn, enables gender balance in the judiciary to be further improved. When these women judges actually engage in active mentoring of younger colleagues, the symbolic paves the way for the practical.

Fourth, women judges are likely to have more empathy with women litigants and witnesses, including victims of crime, and may thus provide a better courtroom experience for these participants in the justice system. Fifth, women judges can educate and civilise their male colleagues by not allowing sexist comments, stereotyping and gender bias to go unquestioned.

Sixth, women judges bring a gendered sensibility to the process of decision-making and can thus alter the outcomes of cases. This, in turn, is based on two main theories. The first is that all judges bring their life experiences to the process of judging, thus, the inclusion of women's experiences will make law more representative of the variety of human experience. The second is that women judge "in a different voice", that is, they apply a feminine "ethic of care" as opposed to the masculine "ethic of justice".

Work on this paper commenced in early 2017 with the intention of analysing decisions of the Supreme Court on cases involving women's issues during the first five years that it was led by a female chief with an ambitious goal to follow through every five years thereafter. There is no denying that research efforts were inspired by the hope of eventually concluding that not only can women on top make a difference, but that this particular woman indeed made a difference for Philippine society. At about the same time, however, Sereno was already the subject of President Rodrigo Duterte's repeated tirades which commenced when she formally expressed disagreement over the latter's public shaming of government officials, including seven judges, whom he claimed to be involved in the illegal drug trade.[5] Not too long after, Sereno was ousted from office on 11 May 2018[6] thereby making the scope of this present work the entirety of her 5 years, 8 months and 18 days in office and how she may have influenced the Supreme Court in such a short period of time.

The controversial ouster of Sereno deserves a thorough dissection in a separate paper. In the meantime, the present work will proceed to discuss leading jurisprudence on three important women's issues – domestic violence, reproductive health, and rape – during her term. The first two issues on domestic violence and reproductive health reached the Supreme Court through cases that challenged the constitutionality of statutes that provided special privileges for women. The last issue on rape is presented through a series of cases ranging from rape within the intimacy of marriage to rape as a wartime offence against humanity. Convictions for rape, owing to the severity of penalties imposed, are elevated to the Supreme Court on automatic review. Thus, a huge number of rape cases have been decided by the Court within the given period but the specific cases pointed out in this work are those where the decisions were authored by the women justices themselves, or have been concurred in by them in a division of five members, and yet continued to employ unfortunate rape myths, trivialised non-traditional form of sexual assault, failed to invoke the rape shield protection, or failed to recognise the victim's right to adequate compensatory damages.

2013 – Domestic violence and the equal protection clause

Right before the conclusion of Sereno's maiden year as a lead magistrate, the Supreme Court upheld the constitutionality of the Anti-Violence Against Women and Their Children Act of 2004 in the case of Garcia v. Drilon.[7]

The law punishes acts of physical, sexual, and psychological violence, including economic abuse, of women and their children committed by their husbands or intimate partners. The law also provides for the issuance of protection orders, among other remedies. The case was brought before the Supreme Court by a disgruntled husband who questioned the validity of several protection orders issued against him on the ground that these violated the equal protection clause.

The majority opinion penned by Bernabe concluded that the classification was valid because it was "germane to the purpose of the law". She mentioned three reasons that justified the classification: (a) the long history of unequal power relationship between men and women; (b) official statistics that show women as the usual and most likely victims of violence in contrast with the absence of reliable estimates on domestic violence committed against men, and (c) the prevalence of gender bias and prejudice in the justice system.

In a separate concurring opinion, De Castro agreed with Bernabe's conclusion but suggested a higher level of scrutiny than what Bernabe employed which was akin to rational basis review, the lowest in the three-tiered approach to equal protection analysis in American jurisprudence.[8] De Castro wanted to apply an intermediate level of scrutiny because ensuring gender equality and empowering women are important and essential governmental objectives and the classification prescribed by the challenged law is substantially related to their achievement. She argued for substantive equality for women whose disadvantaged position required ameliorative measures.

While either approach will yield the same desirable outcome here, it is the majority opinion's preference for the more deferential rational basis review that sets a jurisprudential precedent. Future legislation that favour men based on gender stereotypes could easily survive this lowest level of scrutiny. Sadly, Sereno concurred with Bernabe and not with De Castro.

2014 – Reproductive health and religious freedom

On the second year of Sereno's term, the Supreme Court decided three important cases involving women's issues.

The Responsible Parenthood and Reproductive Health Act of 2012 provided universal access to contraceptives and reproductive health services for Filipinos. The law stopped short of decriminalising abortion but was nonetheless met with widespread protest by various pro-life and pro-family movements. On 8 April 2014, the Supreme Court upheld the constitutionality of the law in the case of Imbong v. Ochoa,[9] but broke much of its teeth.

More specifically, the Supreme Court struck down a provision that allowed a woman to undergo reproductive health procedures without the consent of her husband, or her parents, if she is still a minor. According to the majority opinion written by Associate Justice Jose Mendoza, the questioned provision tends to "wreck the family as a solid social institution". Giving one spouse unbridled discretion instead of requiring mutual consent "will drive a wedge between the husband and the wife, possibly result in bitter animosity, and endanger the marriage and the family". On the other hand, he stressed that a "minor still needs the comfort, care, advice and guidance of her own parents".

The majority opinion significantly watered down the ability of women to seek reproductive health services freely and as they deem fit. Sereno, as well as four other justices, wrote concurring and dissenting opinions.

Sereno stressed that the law does not prohibit joint-decision making but reinforces genuine consultation between spouses when they have equal rights to decide what is best for their future. In case of disagreement, she pointed out that there is no reasonable solution except to respect the right of the spouse who will undergo the procedure to decide what's best for himself or herself. The human right to bodily autonomy is not surrendered upon marriage. Similarly, the law does not preclude a daughter from seeking her parents' advice before undergoing reproductive health procedures nor are her parents prevented from giving this to her. There is nothing in the law that provides for the extinguishment of parental authority nor its take-over by the State.

In writing her opinion in Filipino instead of the customary English, Sereno appears to have intended to reach as many of her countrymen as possible on issues of extreme importance to the Filipino people. Though momentarily drowned by conservative voices in the majority, it is hoped that her articulate dissent will, at some future time, offer a platform for a more liberating view of women's right to bodily autonomy.

2014 – Rape within marriage

The next significant decision came out a few days after on 21 April 2014. In the case of People v. Edgar Jumawan,[10] the Supreme Court upheld the conviction of the accused for raping his wife. Not too long ago, the prevailing view was that marriage was equivalent to perpetual consent to sexual relations. This was effectively erased when the Court proclaimed in this case that "the human rights of women include their right to have control over and decide freely and responsibly matters related to their sexuality, including sexual and reproductive health, free of coercion, discrimination and violence." Women do not surrender these inalienable human rights by contracting marriage.

Nonetheless, the Supreme Court was not contented with women's right to control their own sexuality as rationale for its decision. Instead, it condemned marital rape because it is a violation of the husband's vow to act as his "wife's refuge from cruelty". In utter display of romantic paternalism, the decision enumerated the duties of a husband "to love, cherish and protect his wife, to give her a home, to provide her with the comforts and the necessities of life within his means, to treat her kindly and not cruelly or inhumanely". It also stressed that "he is bound to honor her" and that "it is his duty not only to maintain and support her, but also to protect her from oppression and wrong". This line of reasoning only perpetuates the notion that women are by nature weak and inferior and thus need protection from men. It is very sad that the reasoning of the Court resembled a chivalrous knight in shining armour out to save a damsel in distress.

Moreover, the decision strongly emphasised that sexual intimacy is an integral part of marriage because it is the "spiritual and biological communion that achieves the marital purpose of procreation," as if marriage has no other equally valid motivation. The decision went further by advising men that while they cannot resort to violence or coercion when their wives refuse to engage in sexual intimacy, they may seek nullification of marriage on the basis that such refusal constitutes psychological incapacity to fulfil an essential marital obligation.

Associate Justice Bienvenido Reyes wrote this decision for a division of five members but, with two women – Sereno and De Castro – also in the same division, the phraseology of the decision leaves much to be desired.

2014 – Rape as a crime against humanity

The third decision, Vinuya v. Romulo, was promulgated on 12 August 2014.[11]

The petition was initiated by a group of elderly women who suffered sexual violence in the hands of the Japanese Imperial Army during the Second World War.

The women claimed that they have repeatedly approached various executive departments to assist them in filing claims against Japanese officials who approved the establishment of comfort women stations in the country but were declined assistance because the Philippines already received the full amount of war damages stipulated in its bilateral reparations agreement with Japan.

The Supreme Court dismissed the case on technical grounds. It ruled that it cannot encroach upon the power to determine foreign relations policies which belongs to the executive branch. It added that the executive branch did not commit grave abuse of discretion in declining to take up the petitioners' cause because the country's receipt of compensation entailed a waiver of future claims.

Sereno concurred but wrote in no uncertain terms that the suffering of the Filipinos, especially the petitioners, during the Second World War should not be forgotten. She spoke lengthily on the unfortunate story of the Philippines' attempts to secure appropriate war reparations and how, as a young republic, it was compelled by global forces to accept much less than it deserved. She said we must learn from this experience and "forge the elements that will make the Philippine state strong" enough to protect its people and safeguard their well-being.

She took the opportunity to remind public officials of "the trust the Filipino people have reposed in them to ensure their well-being, address their sufferings, and promote the rule of law within the national and international sphere." She stressed that it is a core duty of every public official to ensure that "every Filipino will attain justice and will be guaranteed full respect for human rights."

Finally, she somehow suggested that under the 1949 Geneva Conventions, the claim of the petitioners may have some leg to stand on should "they bring the same to an appropriate forum or through a proper recourse," hence, the dismissal of the current petition based on technicalities should not be "taken as a definitive ruling on the merits of the claims of the petitioners".

The Chief Justice was sending a very strong message albeit primed with diplomatic prudence.

2015 – Civil indemnity and award of damages for rape survivors

On 6 July 2015, the Supreme Court upheld the conviction of the accused in the case of People v. Jerry Palotes.[12] The victim, who was a 14-year old minor with mental abilities equivalent to that of an 8-year old, gave birth to a child as a result of the rape. The accused attempted to discredit the victim by claiming that she had been seen by neighbours in the company of other men. Confident that somebody else fathered the victim's child, the accused even asked the trial court to order paternity testing. Unfortunately for him, the DNA examination confirmed filiation.

The Supreme Court ordered the accused to pay civil indemnity, moral damages and exemplary damages in the amount of PHP 100,000.00 each.[13]

Under the current state of jurisprudence, this uniform amount is awarded to all rape survivors, whether or not the crime resulted in pregnancy.

People v. Palotes offered the perfect opportunity to review this policy that appears to ignore the additional burdens – financial, physical and psychological – heaped upon a rape survivor who gets pregnant and delivers a child. The various expenses needed for safe delivery as well as for pre- and post-natal care certainly calls for a greater award of civil indemnity. The additional burden upon the victim in this case who now faces the sole responsibility of raising a child despite her own physical immaturity and mental difficulties calls for an even greater amount of moral and exemplary damages.

The decision in People v. Palotes was likewise silent on the issue of child support despite the fact that paternity over the child was established with certainty through DNA examination. In cases where an accused attempts to deny paternity as part of defence theory, it is not uncommon to see courts sweeping the issue under the rug – convicting the accused while casually setting aside the fact of pregnancy for not being an element of the crime. But, such attitude is not necessary in the present case where paternity has been ascertained scientifically. There should be no room for worry over the possibility of rewarding rapists with parental rights contrary to the interests of their victims. While Art. 345 of the Revised Penal Code provides that a person convicted of rape should also be sentenced to pay child support, this does not result in parental authority which is vested in the mother by Art. 176 of the Family Code.

This grievously insensitive decision was written by De Castro for a division of five members which included both Sereno and Bernabe concurring. People v. Palotes attracts interest because three women magistrates who also happened to be mothers appear to have closed their eyes to the unimaginable distress and hardship that unexpected motherhood has brought to a minor with mental disabilities.

2016 – The rape shield law

The case of People v. Roberto Batuhan and Ashley Lacturan[14] was decided by the Supreme Court on 13 August 2016 in an opinion authored by Sereno herself and concurred in by both De Castro and Bernabe.

Convicted for robbery with rape, the accused attempted to cast doubt upon the reliability of the medical report submitted by the prosecution because the victim admitted to having sexual intercourse with her boyfriend before her physical examination by the attending physician.

Sereno dismissed the argument for being "insufficient to negate the clear and convincing testimony of the victim". More importantly, she pointed out that a "medical report is not indispensable to a prosecution for rape" because the "absence of genital injury does not at all mean that a victim was not sexually assaulted".

The Chief Justice was close to a home run but hesitated somewhere along the way. It would have been the perfect opportunity to highlight the decade-old, but never used, rape shield law.

The Rape Victim Assistance and Protection Act of 1998 was enacted for the establishment and operation of rape crisis centres throughout the country to provide assistance to rape victims in litigating their cases and in their recovery. The law also incorporated a rape shield provision which requires that, "evidence of complainant's past sexual conduct, opinion thereof or of his/her reputation shall not be admitted" in a prosecution for rape "unless, and only to the extent that the court finds, that such evidence is material and relevant to the case."

Such widely-phrased exemption renders the protection quite lame. Thus, despite the passage of the law in 1998, the Supreme Court still declared in subsequent cases that on a charge of rape, the victim's character for chastity remains significant. For instance, in Naval v. Panday,[15] the Supreme Court said that "where the willingness of a woman is material, the woman's character as to her chastity is admissible to show whether or not she consented to the man's act". In Civil Service Commission v. Belagan,[16] the Court reiterated an earlier ruling where it expressed doubt and reversed a conviction because "the alleged victim was morally loose and apparently uncaring about her chastity".

The decision in People v. Batuhan and Lacturan could have sounded a wake-up call. The accused was obviously trying to cast doubt upon the credibility of the victim by imputing unchaste behaviour; that she had a boyfriend with whom she admitted to engage in sexual activities and in whose company it appeared typical to be on the streets at 1:30 in the morning, as it were on that woeful day when they fell prey to dreadful criminals. Sadly, Sereno opted not to seize the opportunity to curb the propensity of defence lawyers to use this strategy and sanction the slothfulness of trial judges who remain indifferent to the need to promote gender sensitivity in the courtroom.

2017 – Rape myths

On 15 February 2017, in the case of People v. Juan Richard Tionloc,[17] the Supreme Court shamefully proclaimed that an age gap of six years, where the alleged rape victim was 24 and the accused was 18, negated the presence of force, threat, or intimidation.

The victim here was raped by two young men whom she thought to be her friends. She was casually having a drink with them but on this ill-fated night she had more than enough and fell asleep. She was roused from her slumber when the first rape was being perpetrated but was unable to resist nor shout for help as she cried helplessly out of fear. She knew that a knife was lying at a nearby table which could be used to further harm her. The second rape transpired immediately after the first. Still dizzy, afraid and now shivering due to the first rape, she again failed to manifest resistance other than attempting to move her body.

The trial court was convinced that the testimony of the victim was consistent with human nature and the normal course of things. The Court of Appeals agreed to this finding of credibility. However, the Supreme Court believed otherwise, digressing from the well-settled doctrine that "findings of fact of the trial court and its conclusions based on the said findings are accorded high respect, if not conclusive effect, especially when affirmed by the Court of Appeals".[18]

The Supreme Court decided that the victim's fear for her life "was a mere product of her own imagination" as the knife was not actually brandished upon her. It added that the victim "could have resisted right from the start but she did not and chose not to utter a word or make any sign of rejection" of the sexual advances. The Court interpreted her "unexplainable silence" as "tacit consent". It further said that "resistance must be manifested and tenacious. A mere attempt to resist is not the resistance required and expected of a woman defending her virtue, honor and chastity."

It is ironic to see the Supreme Court taking a journey far back in time after acknowledging in fairly recent decisions that "there is no typical form of behavior for a woman when facing a traumatic experience such as a sexual assault"[19] and that "the failure of a rape victim to shout, fight back, or escape from the scoundrel is not tantamount to consent or approval because the law imposes no obligation to exhibit defiance or present proof of struggle".[20] In People v. Tionloc, however, the Supreme Court imputed fault upon the victim for voluntarily engaging in a drinking session in the house of one of the offenders. The Court even chided the victim for being "used to drinking liquor" and concluded that the "degree of dizziness or shivering was not as grave as she portrayed it to be" because she managed to stand up and walk home after the incident.

Associate Justice Mariano del Castillo wrote this outrageous decision that blamed and shamed the rape victim. None among Sereno, De Castro and Bernabe dared to dissent despite forming a majority in a division of five.

2017 – Forcible insertion of a finger in a woman's vagina is not rape

Under the Revised Penal Code, the crime of rape is committed by a man who shall have "carnal knowledge" of a woman against her will, or under circumstances that deprived her of reason. The criminal element of forced sexual intercourse was expanded by the legislature in 1997 to include the act of inserting a penis into another person's mouth or anal orifice, or any instrument or object, into the genital or anal orifice of another person. This was defined as rape by sexual assault that carried a significantly lower penalty (imprisonment for 6 years and 1 day up to 12 years) than that prescribed for the traditional act that constituted rape (imprisonment for 20 years and 1 day up to 40 years).

After two decades, the Supreme Court was confronted with the case of People v. Noel Caoili where the accused was found to have satisfied his lust by forcibly inserting his finger into the vagina of the victim. The Supreme Court, speaking through Associate Justice Noel Tijam, ruled that this was neither rape in its traditional sense, nor rape by sexual assault. Instead, it downplayed the offence as a mere act of lasciviousness punishable by imprisonment for 6 months and 1 day up to 6 years.

The three women justices concurred with this insensitive opinion that ignored the pain and horror inflicted by the accused upon his victim, his daughter of tender years. It is shameful that these women justices chose to trivialise such beastly act while two male justices took the cudgels for the minor victim.

In his dissenting opinion, Associate Justice Samuel Martires pointed out that limiting the concept of carnal knowledge solely to penile penetration is contrary to human experience. For his part, Associate Justice Marvic Leonen strongly lamented how the Court has turned "blind to the many ways that women's bodies are defiled by the patriarchy".

Discussion

This project was prepared with high hopes over the great potential that rested on the pen of the first woman Chief Justice of the Philippine Supreme Court. Research was pursued with inspiration from the numerical advantage of having three women in the highest court of the land whose combined voices have the potential to make significant rulings on women's issues especially when they constitute majority in a division of five members. Indeed, the Chief Justice manifested commendable grit in registering a meaningful dissent in Imbong v. Ochoa, where she championed women's autonomy over their bodies, and when she wrote a provocative concurrence in Vinuya v. Romulo, where she gave hope to women who suffered wartime atrocities despite the dismissal of their petition based on technicalities. However, she missed an opportunity to put the rape shield law into good use in People v. Batuhan and Lacturan, a majority opinion that she authored. Her silent concurrence was also disappointing in Garcia v. Drilon, where the majority opinion favoured rational basis review over a higher level of scrutiny for gender-based classification; in People v. Jumawan, where a conviction for marital rape was anchored on romantic paternalism; in People v. Palotes, where additional compensatory damages were not considered for a rape victim who delivered a child; in People v. Tionloc where acquittal was based on rape myths; and in People v. Caoli where the Court refused to call rape by its ugly name.

Sereno's appointment as Chief Justice witnessed the symbolic arguments forwarded by Rosemary Hunter coming into fruition. By shattering the glass ceiling, she served as a powerful source of inspiration and encouragement for more women to enter and excel in the legal profession. Raised by humble, working class parents, her assumption of the highest judicial post was a rare triumph of meritocracy over kinship politics that commonly played a huge role both in the election and appointment of women to high government positions in the Philippines.[21]

The symbolic gains, however, were short-lived. Her controversial ouster widely believed to be orchestrated by the current administration of President Duterte significantly eroded the people's faith in the Supreme Court for its blatant failure to protect its independence from the powerful arm of the Chief Executive. Equality of opportunity crumbled to pieces as a young, brilliant, and hardworking Chief Justice was ousted simply because she earned the ire of her seniors. Women must again temper their aspirations lest they become too successful, too soon.

On the other hand, the practical arguments did not yield as much promise, as seen in the rape cases where Sereno seemingly tolerated the inappropriate language and ludicrous reasoning of her male colleagues. Sereno also seemed oblivious to the fact that her colleagues were withholding legal reliefs otherwise available to rape victims. Sereno's acquiescence on occasions when she could have otherwise raised objections invite further research into the power dynamics that animated the Supreme Court during the relevant time.

As for the sixth substantive argument, Sereno inconsistently manifested strong gendered sensibility in Imbong v. Ochoa, retained some good measure in Vinuya v. Romulo, but revealed discouraging paucity in Garcia v. Drilon. In any event, while her feminist reasoning in Imbong v. Ochoa and Vinuya v. Romulo may not have made immense impact presently, the same could very well be the "voice of the future".[22]

Conclusion

The members of the Philippine Supreme Court "hold office during good behavior until they reach the age of 70 or become incapacitated to discharge the duties of their office".[23] Appointed at the age of 52, Sereno was supposed to be Chief Justice for 18 years, effectively erasing any chance at succession for her colleagues who were all destined to retire ahead of her. Seniority is customarily honoured when appointing a Chief Justice but President Aquino defied tradition when he chose Sereno, the second most junior member of the Court. President Aquino was candid about his intention of giving the young Chief Justice all the time that she needed to institute reforms in the judiciary, indirectly ascribing inefficiencies upon other members he strongly perceived as beholden to the previous administration that appointed them.[24] True enough, Sereno spearheaded several projects aimed at improving productivity at various levels of the judiciary but her zeal did not sit well with colleagues who could not get over the irony of having to call a young, female academic with barely two years of experience in the judiciary as chief magistrate, while their own illustrious careers spanned decades in various courts.

While court deliberations are strictly hidden from public view, it was not difficult for avid observers to catch some tell-tale signs of disharmony within the Court such as the repeated absence of the bypassed senior justices during symbolic occasions including the oath-taking ceremony of the Chief Justice before the President[25] and her public address on the occasion of the 112th year of the Supreme Court, the first celebration of the Court's anniversary under her leadership.[26] Their absences were also documented during more casual occasions that called for their show of support such as the regular flag-raising ceremony at the Supreme Court grounds on Monday mornings.[27] For her part, Sereno may have unintentionally allowed a peek into how she was being treated by her colleagues when she gave a truly revealing answer after being asked, five years into her term, on how she dealt with being a female Chief Justice: "Rule number 1, don't ever allow yourself to be bullied".[28]

Renowned Filipino philosopher, Emerita Quito, has this very interesting insight that may serve as a possible explanation for the alienation that Sereno experienced from her peers:

> There is something strange in the very way we [Filipinos] look upon success. A person is not supposed to exert effort at the expense of sanity. We ridicule a person who teaches himself how to think and label him *Tasio*, the philosopher. We warn persons not to learn too much lest they be like Jose Rizal who was executed at the *Luneta* in 1896.[29] Assertiveness is frowned upon because it smacks of pride and ruthlessness. Success to the Filipino, must come naturally; it should not be induced or artificially contrived. One should not be successful at an early age because that would mean exertion and hard work. Success must come very late in life, if it is to come at all.[30]

Aside from achieving so much at a young age, Sereno was also perceived as an outsider in an old boys' club. A well-respected educator and political analyst believes that issues raised against her management style could have been easily ignored, or forgiven, had she been one of the boys. After all, former chiefs had their own shortcomings but were granted much leeway, because they were men. Sadly, Sereno was not only an outsider insofar as her male colleagues were concerned, she was also openly despised by one of her female colleagues, De Castro, who consistently offered opposition at every turn.[31]

Did this unhappy backdrop affect the votes cast by the Chief Justice in the cases discussed? It may be interesting to recall the case of Garcia v. Drilon where the Court upheld the validity of gender-based classification using a rational basis standard of review through a majority opinion authored by Bernabe and concurred in by Sereno. De Castro argued in a separate concurring opinion for a heightened standard of review.

A feminist judge would prefer De Castro's opinion over that of Bernabe's. However, De Castro made things difficult for Sereno, as both of them later admitted.[32] Meanwhile, Bernabe never participated in the seemingly coordinated boycotts against Sereno. In the 2017 Christmas gathering of Supreme Court employees, the last for the embattled Chief, Bernabe gamely joined Sereno on the dance floor while eleven of their colleagues snubbed the party.[33] Perhaps, Sereno opted to take the side of a friendlier female colleague by concurring with Bernabe. At the same time, she neither supported nor contradicted De Castro. After all, the latter was Chair of the Committee on Gender Responsiveness in the Judiciary and President of the Philippine Women Judges Association. Sereno may have felt it better to leave the advocacy to De Castro to buy some peace.

In the meantime, a similar pattern may be read from Sereno's concurrence with Associate Justices Reyes and del Castillo who authored the decisions in People v. Jumawan and People v. Tionloc, respectively. Like Bernabe, they did not participate in the childish boycotts. They were, after all, not among the top contenders leapfrogged by Sereno's appointment. The same can be said for Associate Justice Tijam who authored the decision in People v. Caoili five months after his appointment. Faced with formidable challenges in leading senior colleagues who rejected her outright, Sereno may have chosen to mitigate the stressful situation by preserving a more amicable relationship with those seated by the less senior side of the bench. At the end of the day, this theory over what may have happened does not live up to the high expectations of the Philippine Commission on Women.

In sum, Sereno's term appears to have been preoccupied with instituting ambitious administrative reforms while managing hurt egos. One cannot help but think of greater possibilities had Sereno not been constrained to walk on egg-shells. Had there been enough respect for her leadership, she could have devoted greater effort towards her more substantive duty of decision-making rather than trying to achieve smooth interpersonal relations within the Court. At best, her dissent in Imbong v. Ochoa managed to push for women's reproductive health in an unconventional way for while she was unable to convince her own colleagues, she spoke directly to the sovereign people by writing her opinion in the language that they can fully understand so that future generations may decide for themselves when the appropriate time comes.

Notes

1. 1987 Philippine Constitution, Art.VIII, Secs. 1, 4, 9.
2. Sereno co-authored a book entitled Gender Analysis of Philippine Laws published in 1989 by the National Commission on the Role of Filipino Women, which was eventually renamed as the Philippine Commission on Women.
3. Philippine Commission on Women (2012) Sereno will make hopeful years for women's access to justice, 28 August. Available at: http://pcw.gov.ph/article/sereno-will-make-hopeful-years-women%E2%80%99s-access-justice
4. Rosemary, H. (2015) More than just a different face? Judicial diversity and decision-making, *Current Legal Problems*, p. 119.
5. Lorena, N. (2018) The many times Duterte and Sereno clashed, *Rappler*, 20 May. Available at: https://www.rappler.com/newsbreak/iq/202763-timeline-maria-lourdes-sereno-rodrigo-duterte-clashes

6. Villamor, F. (2018) Philippines' top judge took on Duterte. Now, she's out, *The New York Times*, 11 May. Available at: https://www.nytimes.com/2018/05/11/world/asia/philippines-chief-justice-rodrigo-duterte.html
7. 699 SCRA 352 (2013).
8. The rational basis test is the most deferential level of judicial review where classification is readily sustained by the courts for as long as such is rationally related to a legitimate state interest. Laws that facially discriminate against a "suspect class" (e.g. race), however, are subject to strict scrutiny. The government must prove that the classification is necessary to achieve a compelling state purpose. Finally, laws that affect a "quasi-suspect class" (e.g. gender) receive an intermediate level of scrutiny. The classification must be substantially related to an important government purpose for it to be sustained.
9. 721 SCRA 146 (2014).
10. 722 SCRA 108 (2014).
11. 732 SCRA 595 (2014).
12. 761 SCRA 633 (2015).
13. At the current exchange rate of USD 1 = PHP 53, the amount of P100,000.00 would translate to more or less USD 1,886.79 only.
14. G.R. No. 219830, August 3, 2016.
15. 321 SCRA 290 (1999).
16. 483 Phil. 601 (2004).
17. G.R. No. 212193, February 15, 2017.
18. See, e.g. People v. Iroy, 614 SCRA 245 (2010).
19. People v. Manicat, 711 SCRA 284 (2013).
20. People v. Linsie, 711 SCRA 125 (2013).
21. The late Senator Miriam Defensor Santiago described Sereno's appointment as "a triumph of superior intellect over shabby politics". Miriam praises P. Noy's first appointment to SC, *ABS-CBN News*, August 14, 2010. Available at: http://news.abs-cbn.com/nation/08/14/10/miriam-praises-pnoys-first-appointment-sc
22. L'Heureux-Dube, C. (2000) The dissenting opinion: voice of the future?, *Osgoode Hall Law Journal*, 495.
23. Supra n.1, at Art. VIII, Sec. 11. They may also be removed from office on impeachment for, and conviction of, culpable violation of the Constitution, treason, bribery, graft and corruption, other high crimes, or betrayal of public trust (Art. XI, Sec. 2).
24. Dizon, D. (2012) Sereno is new Chief Justice, *ABS-CBN News*, 24 August. Available at: https://news.abs-cbn.com/nation/08/24/12/sereno-new-chief-justice
25. Burgonio, T. J. (2012) Aquino swears in PH's first woman Chief Justice, *The Philippine Daily Inquirer*, 25 August. Available at: https://newsinfo.inquirer.net/257566/sereno-takes-oath-as-new-chief-justice
26. Supreme Court Justices Boycott Sereno 'unity' speech, *The Manila Times*, 11 July 2013. Available at: https://www.manilatimes.net/supreme-court-justices-boycott-sereno-unity-speech/9039/
27. Torres, T. (2012) Justices skip flag ceremony with sereno for third time, *The Philippine Daily Inquirer*, 17 September. Available at https://newsinfo.inquirer.net/272146/justices-skip-flag-ceremony-with-sereno-for-third-time
28. Buan, L. (2017) "Do not be afraid to be minority": Sereno, 5 Years on, *Rappler*, 27 August. Available at: https://www.rappler.com/nation/180185-chief-justice-sereno-5-years-sc-impeachment-challenges
29. Jose Rizal is the national hero of the Philippines. Filosofo Tacio is one of the characters in his novel, Noli Me Tangere.

30. Quito, E. (1988) The ambivalence of Filipino traits and values, *Karunungan: Sophia*, 5 (1), pp. 42, 43.
31. Buan, L. (2017) Sereno impeachment: cracks in the Supreme Court, *Rappler*, 12 December. Available at: https://www.rappler.com/newsbreak/in-depth/191150-sereno-impeachment-cracks-supreme-court
32. The grudge: Sereno says De Castro won't forgive her for accepting Chief Justice post, *ABS-CBN News*, April 9, 2018. Available at: https://news.abs-cbn.com/news/04/09/18/the-grudge-sereno-says-de-castro-wont-forgive-her-for-accepting-chief-justice-post
33. Macairan, E. (2017) Sereno dances away impeach woes, *The Philippine Star*, 15 December. Available at: https://www.philstar.com/headlines/2017/12/15/1768872/chief-justice-sereno-dances-away-impeach-woes

Disclosure statement

No potential conflict of interest was reported by the author.

The Judicial Service Commission and the appointment of women: more to it than meets the eye

Tabeth Masengu

ABSTRACT
The Judicial Service Commission (JSC) in South Africa was established in response to a pre-democratic era appointment system rich in patronage, opaqueness, and invariably, inequality. The use of judicial appointment bodies has been recommended by the Commonwealth Latimer House Principles, as a method of preserving judicial independence. However, not much research has been conducted into whether there is an absence of patronage and power dynamics when judicial appointment bodies replace executive type of appointments. This paper suggests that the introduction of appointment bodies does not eradicate privilege and power dynamics as some might believe. Rather, it creates a different type of dynamic that can be harmful for women.

Introduction

The Commonwealth Latimer House Principles on Three Branches of Government declare that states should have an appropriate independent process for judicial appointments and preferably a judicial appointments commission for this purpose (Commonwealth 2003).[1] The Cape Town Principles also emphasise that if commissions are to make a contribution to creating and sustaining an independent judiciary, such commissions must themselves be manifestly independent, and suitably composed and resourced (Cape Town Principles on the Role of Independent Commissions in the Selection and Appointment of Judges 2016).[2] Since 1987, models for judicial appointments commissions have been developed and improved, in part because of a desire for a more professionalised and transparent selection process (Davis and Williams 2003). South Africa is a commonwealth state, which formerly used the Westminster judicial appointment system until 1994. The Westminster system was shrouded in secrecy, lending itself to what is often referred to as the "tap on the shoulder" appointment system (Hale 2006). Prior to 1994, the Minister of Justice made appointments. Sometimes this was on the recommendation of the Chief Justice and Judge President, with the President only acting as a rubber stamp (Wesson and Du Plessis 2008). These appointments were from the ranks of senior counsel and were invariably white and male.

When the Judicial Service Commission was introduced in 1994, the aim was to have a process that was more legitimate, open and less likely to be abused by the executive (Du Bois 2006). By and large the JSC has been successful in achieving this aim. In addition, there have been great improvements in gender and race representation over the years and greater involvement of different stakeholders in the process (Oxtoby and Masengu 2017). The percentage of black judges increased from 1.4% in 1994 to 67% as of September 2017.[3] However, gender transformation has long lagged, with the representation of women on the bench increasing from 1.2% to 37% over the same period.[4] It has been suggested that appointment commissions may increase judicial gender equity, because patronage plays a smaller role in commissions than it does, in systems where one person is responsible for making appointments (Iyer 2013, p.102; Rackley 2009). However to date, current literature has focused on the modalities of the appointment process and the responsibility that appointers have to diversify the judiciary (Patterson 2006; Iyer 2013; Oxtoby and Masengu 2017).

This has resulted in a blind-spot that this essay tackles. Herein, I argue that judicial appointment bodies and their processes are not free from partiality, patronage and power dynamics–they just appear in a different form. I posit that it is necessary to identify the challenges of appointment processes that utilise JSCs, if we are to continue to strive for gender equity on the bench. I construct my argument with the aid of data from 20 interviews conducted in South Africa, in the period October 2016 to August 2017. The interview participants (herein referred to as interviewees) included women judges of different seniority, legal professionals, JSC members, members of Civil Society Organisations (CSOs) and journalists. Interview data are supplemented with participant observations of the judicial interview process in South Africa and academic literature. To provide a holistic picture of the nature of the challenges that I refer to, this paper commences with a brief contextual background of the South African system. An overview of the judicial appointments process and the composition of the JSC follows. I then discuss three sites of partiality, power and patronage as observed in the JSC process– specifically regarding the appointment of women. These are the politicisation of interviews, acting experience as a form of patronage and finally the recruitment process as a site of power and partiality.

Background

The South African JSC is created by the Constitution of the Republic of South Africa 1998 (herein referred to as the South African Constitution) and is mandated to recommend[5] candidates for appointment to the Superior Courts.[6] One of the JSC's responsibilities is transformation of the judiciary which requires changes in the way judges are appointed, a change in the demographic of judges and a change in underlying attitudes of the judiciary, to see them embracing the principles of a fundamentally new legal order (Wesson and Du Plessis

2008). The regulations governing the JSC's procedure require that the JSC publicly announce judicial vacancies, call for nominations from the public and interview candidates in public (Oxtoby and Masengu 2017).[7] This is different from the Apartheid era system, where appointments were made secretly, which resulted in a judiciary entirely lacking in diversity in terms of demographic representation, social background and professional career paths (Du Bois 2006).

Overview of the composition of the JSC

The composition of the JSC is outlined in section 178 of the Constitution. Chaired by the Chief Justice, it has between 23 and 25 members, who include judges, practicing lawyers and politicians. This includes six members of the National Assembly, of whom three are from the opposition, and four permanent delegates of the National Council of Provinces (NCOP) – who are all from the ruling party, the African National Congress (ANC).[8] The Minister of Justice and Constitutional Development is also a member of the JSC and sometimes the Premier of the province or an alternate also sits in.[9] With four other presidential appointees, there could potentially be sixteen members who are politicians and/or designated by politicians. Du Bois has suggested that this is to ensure that appointments are the product of collective decision-making, involving all major interested parties (Du Bois 2006). However, there were different opinions from the interviewees on the utility of having many politicians on the JSC.

Those who are against the composition argued that the large number of politicians did not augur well for what is meant to be a professional process. They also opined that politicians do not ask the right questions, that different interests amongst politicians affected the entire process and that their mandate, even in a legal process would always be political, because they were incapable of fully shedding their "political hats".[10] Counter arguments to these were that politicians played a vital role by asking non-legal questions and that opposition members provided checks and balances.[11] At least three interviewees mentioned that the drafters of the Constitution must have had good reason to include the large political compliment and that politicians have their feet and ears on the ground. The analysis below examines the political presence on the JSC and instances where politicians have wielded their powers negatively. The subsequent two sections will then highlight instances where patronage and privilege have been used to the detriment of women.

When politics is present in interviews: utilising power

To examine the dynamics of power present in the judicial interviews process, I use two case scenarios. One explores the effect of the judgment in *Southern African Litigation Centre v Minister of Justice and Others*, on identified interviews.[12] The other scenario considers the interview of a judge who made a ruling which concerned the conviction of a member of the ruling party.

The Al-Bashir judgment overshadows a historical moment

A legal professional opined that political debate often invaded judicial interviews, which was a worrying trend.[13] A blatant instance of this occurred during what was meant to be a historical moment for proponents of gender equity on the bench. On 9 July 2015, four candidates were interviewed for a Constitutional Court vacancy. They were all women and so was Justice Mandisa Maya, the first woman to ever be nominated for the position of Deputy President of the Supreme Court of Appeal.[14] This moment was particularly poignant because critics of transformation had argued that merit was being sacrificed at the altar of transforming the judiciary (Masengu 2015b). Yet all five women interviewed had strong jurisprudential records, stellar careers and had very impressive CV's.

Unfortunately, instead of focusing on these attributes, a substantial amount of time was devoted to assessing whether the candidates had the potential to make "dangerous judgments." The desire to assess this aspect came primarily from the Minister of Justice in reaction to a High Court decision, that held that government had failed to comply with an earlier court order to detain Sudanese President Omar al –Bashir on the arrest warrant issued by the International Criminal Court (ICC). The court held further that the government had ignored its constitutional obligations when it allowed Al-Bashir to leave. This was a damning verdict for government and a source of political tension prior to the interviews. Yet the blatant inferences that judges should "know their place" still came as a surprise, especially because the decision in question was not delivered by any of the two courts that the candidates were vying for.

As I observed the interviews, some members of the commission became increasingly uncomfortable. As one journalist put it:

> the Minister of Justice kept pushing this thing about consequences and how judges should consider the consequences of their judgements on the outside world, kind of setting the impression that judges should like in a way be compromised in making their decisions. The Minister of Justice has not been, I go as far as saying independent in a way and he has been very biased.[15]

The Chief Justice tried to defend the judiciary which resulted in moments where the interviews were more about the tension between the judiciary and the executive, than about the candidate being interviewed (Masengu 2015b). The political agitation present in the interviews, was essentially about power. The power that the executive has, the power that they felt was being exercised unjustifiably by the courts and the power of politics to enter a judicial interview and dominate what is meant to be a professional process. In the end, the historical moment that might have been the best exhibition of women candidates' jurisprudential prowess, was wrongly over-shadowed by political anger at what was considered as a court's overreach. It was implied that judges shouldn't hand down negative decisions that could influence political governance and international relations.

Nonetheless, other interviews have shown that politician's unhappiness with judgments is not limited to issues of national governance.

When cases a judge has heard are used against them

Judges preside over all manner of cases and a judge sitting alone rarely chooses which cases to hear. For judge Violet Phatsoane, her decision in a particular case earned her the ire of politicians in one of her JSC interviews.[16] Judge Phatsoane had sentenced former Northern Cape ANC provincial chairperson John Block to 15 years imprisonment, after finding him guilty of corruption and money laundering following an arduous four-year trial.[17] Members of the ANC took her to task, by inferring that she had been partial and that Mr Block did not deserve his sentence.[18] Former Minister Faith Muthambi further added that Phatsoane's refusal to recuse herself from the trial showed bias.[19] Mr Nyambi an ANC NCOP member, on more than one occasion stated that Judge Phatsoane had been compromised and suggested she had acted in in a legally reprehensible manner. The discussion was only terminated when opposition MP Julius Malema stated that the case was *sub judice* because it had gone on appeal.

This interview was a fitting example of what one legal professional described as instances where "political questions are not so much on what is expected of a judge, but more like what it expected of a political activist". She added "when you are judge you are not a political activist".[20] As a frequent observer of the JSC interviews when I saw Judge Phatsoane's name on the shortlist, I anticipated that she would not have a smooth interview because of this particular case. Over the years I have discerned that any politically contentious judgments always come to haunt the person who made a decision that was not in the favour of the ruling party–the ANC.[21] The line of questioning would be understandable if the questioner sought a better understanding of how the judge reasoned in coming to their decision. Instead, the interview was another example of how politicians wield their power in interviews to undermine a candidate's application.

An argument could be made that a politician on the JSC represents their constituency and invariably the party that they belong to. Therefore, politicians cannot be expected to shy away from interrogating candidates when there is a political interest at stake. Yet Dodek and Devlin posit that for a judicial appointment process to be independent:

> processes and procedures must be designed in such a way that participants in the selection process do not operate as, or perceive themselves to be, agents/representatives of a constituency. Rather, they are fiduciaries whose responsibility is to select judges who will generate public confidence in the administration of justice. (Devlin and Dodek 2017)

One of the strengths of judicial appointments bodies in comparison to the executive-only type of appointment model, is meant to be independence. In instances such as the one in question, had the politicians acted like fiduciaries rather than agents of their constituency, there would have been less of a need to make the interview about one judgment. Instead by focusing on the judgment the JSC members cast doubt about their independence, because they operated as agents of their constituencies. Judge Phatsoane was not appointed and we are not privy to the reasons why. However, it is certain that such a politically charged interview can only serve to discourage other judges who have ruled against the ANC from applying for promotion.

Patronage – acting experience as a requirement for appointment as a judge

In South Africa, acting judges are appointed to fill temporary vacancies caused by the absence or disability of particular judges (Harms 2010). There is no written requirement that a judicial candidate needs to have acted in the court they are applying for, yet very few candidates have been appointed without it (Mocumie 2017). In principle acting experience is important because it exposes candidates to the rigours of the court and gives them an opportunity to learn how to control the court – while gaining valuable experience in writing judgments.[22] One senior woman judge emphasised how important acting experience was, especially for courts like the Supreme Court of Appeal. She stated:

> In our court, you work in panels and if you have a judge who cannot work with other judges, you can't appoint someone like that to our court. If you have a judge who cannot have his or her judgements interrogated by colleagues, you cannot have someone like that work at our court.[23]

The importance of acting experience was uncontested amongst interviewees. However, there was a unanimous view that the way acting appointments are made is prejudicial – especially to women.

The statistics of acting appointments speak for themselves. In the period of 2010–2016, 6017 acting opportunities(ranging from a week to a few months) were available across the country. Of this total, only 1224 opportunities were given to women, a mere 20% of the opportunities.[24] Women are effectively prejudiced by this situation because acting experience is highly prized by the JSC. I previously argued that acting experience or lack thereof, has been used to disqualify women from ordinary court vacancies and leadership positions (Masengu 2015a). In particular, it has been an obstacle for women to become Judge Presidents– the heads of each provincial court division. This changed with the appointment of Judge Mahube Molemela as the Judge President of the Free State in October 2014 and another woman has since been appointed into a leadership position with no acting experience.[25] However, these are exceptions.

In 2013, at a meeting of esteemed members of the judiciary and legal profession, officials from the department of justice and others, it was agreed that there was a need to scrutinise how acting appointments are made.[26] This is because they had gained the status of "pre-appointment" to the bench. A 2015 report based on five legal sector meetings across the country with various stakeholders, noted that:

> Judge Presidents of the various provincial divisions exercise their discretion on who to appoint in the absence of a guideline or policy. Selections or acting appointments are generally closed processes that lead to acting appointments of candidates who are known to the individuals making the decisions about who to appoint. This results in many interested or suitable candidates not being appointed on an acting basis. (Masengu and Sanger 2015)

In response to the report and other complaints in April 2016, the JSC issued guidelines pertaining to the appointment of acting judges. The guidelines require that a candidate should have been in practice for ten years and must be appropriately qualified (Judicial Service Commission of South Africa 2016), but they do not expound on what appropriately qualified means.

The guidelines also advise courts to have a selection committee for the recommendation of candidates and urge the committee to consider the gender and racial composition of the country, when candidates are being chosen. Nevertheless, there are still discrepancies in how candidates are appointed across the country. One magistrate who has acted before stated that she had no idea how she was identified as a candidate to act in the Free State High Court or on what basis she was selected.[27] An advocate from the Cape Bar offered:

> if I recall there was a communication, there was a request for people to put their names for appointment as acting judges, but it wasn't entirely clear on exactly how that would work. It was, it is not clear on whether it is then the profession that decides whose names go forward.[28]

Differences persist in different provinces. In Gauteng, Judge President Dunstan Mlambo actively seeks women practitioners from the bar and the attorneys' profession and the former Judge President of the Northern Cape, Frans Kgomo had a similar approach.[29] In Kwa-Zulu Natal, a committee headed by the Judge President relies on lists of nominees provided to them by the Bar, Attorneys and the Magistracy.[30] At the Supreme Court of Appeal, one of the methods is for the President of the court to invite Judge Presidents in the country to send her names of judges for acting.[31]

Irrespective of what method is used, it all comes down to the prerogative of the Judge President who leads the division. As one journalist added, "you're in a particular division and you rub the Judge President the wrong way, means that you're not going climb the sort of legal ladder until he moves".[32] One JSC member found that Judge Presidents are biased in how they select candidates and this gives their "chosen" candidates an unfair advantage over others.[33] Another said they have come across candidates with great potential who had not been given an opportunity to act and others who faced obstruction from their divisions.[34]

It could be argued that the JSC are complicit in the acts of patronage if they do not monitor Judge Presidents or call them to account for not giving women enough acting opportunities, The JSC has a very critical role to play in the process, "because an acting stint is very important, important for the institution and it's important for this person who aspires to go and work in that court ultimately".[35] An acting appointment system based on patronage is not useful for the appointment process and it will continue to be an impediment for women.

The recruitment process as an avenue for partiality and power dynamics

The final area for discussion is the recruitment process and the power dynamics that are at play there. The JSC announcement of vacancies, call for nominations and interviews are all public. This is for the purposes of transparency in order to allow the public to observe how judges are appointed. Yet I have identified an area that lacks transparency – the sifting process. When vacancies arise the JSC call for nominations and after about two months, the JSC issues an interview schedule of the shortlisted candidates.[36] However, the information of those who have not been short-listed is never made public. Andrews has questioned how the choices are made, since the names of those who are nominated but not shortlisted, are not published (Andrews 2006). She has questioned whether there could there be any political and other inappropriate influences involved in the decisions (p.569).

The JSC has often said there are not enough women applying for vacancies.[37] However this cannot be contested because we are unaware of the total number of women applying, versus those who are shortlisted. While the JSC sifting subcommittee does assess candidates based on its publicly available criteria for judicial appointments,[38] it does not apply the same stringency as it does in the public interviews.[39] Judge President Mlambo stated that the view in the sub-committee is that if a candidate has a realistic chance, they should be shortlisted. This approach was called into question on 5 March 2015, when the JSC issued a shortlist of people who would be interviewed for various positions in the period 13–17 April. On the list for the position of Judge President of the Limpopo High Court were two names– Judges M F Legodi and E M Makgoba (Judicial Service Commission 2015a). On 11 March six days later, the JSC issued an amended shortlist after the sub-committee consulted with the Chief Justice (Judicial Service Commission 2015b). This time the list had increased to seven candidates which included one-woman candidate, Judge Thokozile Masipa.[40] This amendment was unusual for one reason.

Over the years it has become custom that sitting judges applying for appointment to higher courts are immediately shortlisted, because they clearly meet the minimum for requirements for appointment. The JSC regulations provide that members of the sub-committee must provide the full JSC body with the shortlist, prior to the final list being sent. Within seven days of receipt, JSC members may request that a candidate, who was nominated but did not make the shortlist; be added to the shortlist.[41] In this particular instance the Chief Justice used the JSC regulations to request that the additional judges should be added to the shortlist.[42] The question arises, if sitting judges have not been shortlisted despite what has become common practice, what does this mean for ordinary applicants? Had the Chief Justice not intervened, we would never have known that one woman applied for that vacancy. This also raises questions about how many "suitable" women have been left out by the process.

The number of women shortlisted by the JSC for various vacancies suggests that while progress is being made, there appears to be a shortage of women candidates viewed as appointable (Commission for Gender Equality 2016). Yet I submit that this is debatable if we have no information of how many women are nominated. One argument for not disclosing the long-list is to protect the privacy of the individual concerned (Andrews 2006). Former JSC member Advocate Leah Gcabashe SC stated that the purpose of not publicising the long-list is a way of preventing unsuccessful candidates from feeling disgraced.[43] It is important to protect candidates but when one applies for public office, there is a certain risk that comes with it. This risk may include an intrusion on a candidate's privacy however, that the aim of protecting people's privacy cannot be greater than the aim of ensuring that the process is devoid of suspicion.

The challenge of the current sifting process is that is it open to various influences. The other spectrum of the problem is that if the process is lacking in rigour, this can have its perils for women in another manner. In April 2017, three women candidates were interviewed for one vacancy on the Eastern Cape High Court bench. Only one of them, Ms Sadia Jacobs, had acted for at least nine months.[44] Advocate Vijaylutchmee Reddy had only acted for ten weeks, while Ms Fezeka Monakali had never acted at all. I refer to the previous section on acting appointments where I emphasised the importance of acting experience, if one is seeking permanent appointment. From observation at the interviews, the preferred minimum of acting experience if six months. Therefore, it was obvious during Reddy and Monakali's interviews that they lacked the necessary experience to even be shortlisted for the position. Advocate Reddy was questioned about her lack of High Court exposure in civil cases and her lack of judgments, when she briefly acted on the court. Her interview lasted nine minutes, which is the shortest interview I have observed in my five years of monitoring the JSC.

Ms Monakali's interview lasted longer but was comparably worse than Advocate Reddy's, due to her lack of acting experience and current position as a district magistrate.[45] By her own admission, her current position and workload, did not compare to the High Court, because of the difference in jurisdiction. Apart from lacking extensive judgment writing experience, comments from the legal profession alleged that she was careless, lacked precision in her *ex tempore* judgments and lacked technical competence. Finally, an admission from Ms Monkali that she was using the JSC interview to make the Judge President offer her an acting appointment, proved a nail on the coffin. A synopsis captured the interviews aptly:

> the process did little to advance gender transformation of the judiciary, and that Reddy and Monakali must have felt humiliated by the interview process was palpable – this was no exercise in encouraging women to avail themselves for the high court. It was, rather, just a waste of tax-payers' money that may have crushed the spirit of potential future judges. (Tolsi 2017)

So why were these two candidates allowed to participate in a process that proved professionally embarrassing?

When I made enquiries, I was informed that those two women had initially not been short-listed but once the list was sent out, some JSC members requested that they should be added to the list.[46] The rationale behind this decision is unknown, but the result of the two interviews must have left the candidates questioning themselves. It also did little to improve perceptions that there are not enough women– especially women of colour; qualified to be judges on the bench Not only did the addition of extra candidates to the shortlist in this round prove to be a disadvantage for women, but it also highlighted the challenges of the sifting process.

The process allows for power and partiality in two ways. Firstly, the sub-committee does appear to have the power to not shortlist potentially qualified candidates, as was seen in the Limpopo High Court interview. Secondly, it allows for partiality because there is a possibility that somebody could be left out or added to the list because of their connection to a JSC member. We do not know who has fallen through the cracks or who has not been shortlisted because of a personal objection from a JSC member. What is also debatable is whether the JSC members who asked that Monkali and Reddy be added to the short-list, did so because they genuinely wanted to advance the cause for women. Or whether it was a simply a case of some JSC members partiality, based on personal and /or professional knowledge of the candidates? What is clear, is that the current sifting system can contain partiality and power dynamics that appointment bodies are meant to avoid.

Conclusion

In this paper, I have argued that judicial appointments bodies are not devoid of partiality, patronage and power dynamics. Using three sites, I have highlighted how these dynamics can manifest through politics in interviews, the requirements of acting appointments and the sifting process. I recognise that the JSC has a daunting task ahead of them of transforming the judiciary in both demographics and mind-set, while ensuring that the process remains rigorous, transparent and protective of candidates' dignity. They have made great progress in this regard. There is no single appointment model that is without challenges, and stronger policies and goals need to be articulated to guide appointers (Devlin *et al.* 2000). Therefore, I would recommend the consideration of a more stringent interview process by the JSC. A process that ensures that politicians are confined to matters relating to the actual assessment of a candidate's legal acumen.

Secondly, it is necessary to have a stricter regulation of the acting appointments system. This would require that when recruiting candidates, every division is using a framework that is transparent and equitable, while recognising particular the needs of the court. This framework should include a mandate to have least 50% of the opportunities going to women. Finally, there needs to be a revisiting of the sifting process to ensure that opportunities for partiality and patronage are eliminated. If these issues are not addressed, the advantages of appointing bodies as opposed to executive type appointments will start to diminish. This would be a pity because ultimately, the JSC has changed the nature of judicial appointments and the judges who preside in the country for the better.

Notes

1. Adopted the Heads of State of Commonwealth countries in 2002.
2. The outcome of an international research project which brought together scholars from Canada, Kenya, Malaysia, Nigeria, South Africa and the UK.
3. As per legislation, the term black refers to African, Coloured and Indians.
4. Statistics provided by the Department of Justice and Constitutional Development, on file with the author.
5. Exceptions to this are the appointment of the Chief Justice, Deputy Chief Justice, President and Deputy President of the Supreme Court of Appeal.
6. This refers to the High Courts, Specialist Courts, Supreme Court of Appeal and the Constitutional Court.
7. *JSC Act, 1994 (Act No. 9 of 1994): Procedure of Commission*, Government Gazette No. 7616 Volume 453, 27 March 2003 No. 24596.
8. The NCOP is the lower House of Parliament and the representatives are all from the ruling party.
9. A premier is the political leader of a designated province.
10. Views from a JSC member, a sitting Judge, a retired judge and a senior advocate.
11. Views from a politician, a journalist, and two sitting judges.
12. *Southern African Litigation Centre v Minister of Justice and Others* at http://www.politicsweb.co.za/documents/albashir-salc-vs-the-govt-high-court-judgment.
13. Interview with legal professional V, 12 October 2016.
14. For the Constitutional Court the JSC interviewed Justices Leona Theron, Zukisa Tshiqui, Nonkonsi Mthlantla and Judge Dhaya Pillay.
15. Interview with a journalist, 6 August 2017.
16. Judge of the Northern Cape.
17. See National Director of Public Prosecutions v Scholtz and Others (2027/2012, KS20/2013) [2016] ZANCHC 37 at http://www.saflii.org/za/cases/ZANCHC/2016/37.html.
18. Interview round of 3–7 April, Office of the Chief Justice in Noordwyk, Midrand.

19. There was an allegation that then Judge President Frans Kgomo, had influenced her decision.
20. Interview with a Regional magistrate on 22 October 2016.
21. For instance, in October 2013, Judge Clive Plasket was taken to task over decisions he had made against government in regards to social security in the Eastern Cape.
22. Views from a journalist, a woman judge and Advocate Leah Gcabshe SC, a former member of the JSC.
23. Interview with an anonymous justice, 5 April 2017.
24. Statistics obtained from the Department of Justice and Constitutional Development.
25. Deputy Judge President Patricia Goliath was appointed in May 2016.
26. Paarl conference held by Democratic Governance and Rights Unit
27. Interview with an anonymous legal professional, 12 October 2016.
28. Interview with an advocate of the Cape Bar, 17 July 201
29. Interviews with both Judge Presidents 5–6 April 2017.
30. Address by Judge Kate Pillay at the Kwa-Zulu Natal legal sector Meeting,
31. Interview with a former Supreme Court of Appeal justice, 5 April 2017.
32. Interview with a professional journalist, 5 October 2016.
33. Interview with a JSC member, 18 May 2017.
34. Interview with Honorable Thandi Modise, 15 June 2017.
35. Interview with a senior judge, 11 January 2017.
36. This allows selected organisations and members of the public to comment on the candidates.
37. This was stated by former JSC spokesperson Dumisa Ntsebenza in 2012 and 2013.
38. See https://constitutionallyspeaking.co.za/criteria-used-by-jsc-when-considering-judicial-appointments/.
39. Interview with Judge President Mlambo 6 April 2017.
40. Others were Judges K Makhafola, N F Kgomo, A M L Phatudi and T J Raulinga.
41. Section f 2(ii) of the Regulation Gazette, No. 24596, 27 March 2003.
42. Interview with JSC member, 18 May 2017.
43. Interview on 2 April 2017.
44. JSC interviews held on 6 April 2017.
45. District magistrate is the lowest level of magistrate in the courts.
46. Interview with JSC member, 14 May 2017.

Disclosure statement

No potential conflict of interest was reported by the author.

Funding

This work was supported by Research Foundation of Flanders (FWO) [grant number 2013.0118.01]; Bijzonder Onderzoeksfonds (BOF) FJD is a special research Fund via the University of Ghent [grant number 2016.0001.01].

References

Andrews, P.E. (2006) The South African judicial appointments process, *Osgoode Hall Law Journal*, 44(3), pp. 565–572.

Du Bois, F. (2006) Judicial selection in post-apartheid South Africa, in: K. Malleson and P.H. Russell (Eds) *Appointing Judges in an Age of Judicial Power - Critical Perspectives from Around the World* (Toronto: University of Toronto Press Incorp), pp. 280–312.

Cape Town Principles on the Role of Independent Commissions in the Selection and Appointment of Judges. (2016) Cape Town. Available at: https://www.biicl.org/documents/868_cape_town_principles_-_feb_2016.pdf?showdocument=1.

Commission for Gender Equality. (2016) Lack of Gender Transformation in the Judiciary Investigative Report. Available at: http://www.cge.org.za/wp-content/uploads/2016/12/CGE-Lack-of-Gender-Transformation-in-the-Judiciary-Investigative-Report-.pdf.

Commonwealth. (2003) *Commonwealth (Latimer House) Principles on the Three Branches of Government*. Available at: http://www.cmja.org/downloads/latimerhouse/commprinthreearms.pdf.

Davis, R. & Williams, G. (2003) A century of appointments but only one woman, *Alternative Law Journal*, 28, pp. 54–58.

Devlin, R. & Dodek, A. (2017) The Achilles heel of the Canadian judiciary: the ethics of judicial appointments in Canada, *Legal Ethics*, 20(1), pp. 47–63. Available at: https://doi.org/10.1080/1460728x.2017.1345202.

Devlin, R., Wayne MacKay, A. & Kim, N. (2000) Reducing the democratic deficit: representation, diversity and the Canadian judiciary, or towards a triple P judiciary, *ALberta Law Review*, 38, pp. 734–865. Available at: http://heinonline.org/HOL/Page?handle=hein.journals/alblr38&id=746&div=34&collection=journals.

Hale, B.B. (2006) The appointment and removal of judges: independence and diversity. Sydney, Australia.

Harms, L.T.C. (2010) Transparency and accountability in the judicial appointment process, *Advocate*, 23(2), pp. 36–38. Available at: http://www.sabar.co.za/law-journals/2010/august/2010-august-vol023-no2-pp36-38.pdf.

Iyer, S. (2013) The fleeting benefits of appointments commissions for judicial gender equity, *Commonwealth & Comparative Politics*, 51(1), pp. 97–121. Available at: https://doi.org/10.1080/14662043.2013.749673.

Judicial Service Commission. (2015a) *Shortlisted Candidates- April 2015 Media*. Johannesburg: Office of the Chief Justice Republic of South Africa.

Judicial Service Commission. (2015b) *Shortlisted Candidates for Judicial Positions*. Johannesburg: South African Judicial Service Commission.

Judicial Service Commission Act 9 of 1994, Procedure for Commission. (2003) Department of Justice and Constitutional Development. Available at: http://www.justice.gov.za/legislation/regulations/r2003/2003_r423_gg24596-jsc.pdf.

Judicial Service Commission of South Africa. (2016). *Criteria for acting appointments*. Johannesburg: Office of the Chief Justice Republic of South Africa.

Masengu, T. (2015a) A perspective on women and leadership in the South African judiciary, *South African Journal on Human Rights*, 31(15), pp. 655–666. Available at: http://ipproducts.jutalaw.co.za/nxt/print.asp?NXTScript=nxt/gateway.dll&NXTHost=ipproducts.jutalaw.co.za&d=&multi=0&pb=0&isrc=yes&f=print&.

Masengu, T. (2015b) Small steps in the journey towards gender equality on the South African Bench | OHRH. Oxford Human Rights Hub. 2015. Available at: http://ohrh.law.ox.ac.uk/small-steps-in-the-journey-towards-gender-equality-on-the-south-african-bench/.

Masengu, T. & Sanger, C. (2015) *Legal Sector Meetings on Gender Transformation in the Judicairy*. Cape Town. Available at: http://www.dgru.uct.ac.za/sites/default/files/image_tool/images/103/gender.pdf.

Mocumie, C.B. (2017) Gender Transformation of the Judiciary in South Africa through the Eyes of a Woman Judge. Unpublished.

Oxtoby, C. & Masengu, T. (2017) Who nominates judges? Some issues underlying judicial appointments in South Africa, *Stellenbosch Law Review*, 3, pp. 541–563.

Patterson, A. (2006) The Scottish Judicial Appointments Board: new wine in old bottles, in: *Appointing Judges in an Age of Judicial Power;Critical Perspectives From Around the World* (Toronto: University of Toronto Press Incorp), pp. 13–38.

Rackley, E. (2009) Submission to the Lord Chancellor's Advisory Panel on Judicial Diversity. Durham. Available at: http://www.law.qmul.ac.uk/eji/docs/51452.pdf.

Tolsi, N. (2017) Vijaylutchmee Reddy – judges matter. Judge Matter. Available at: http://www.judgesmatter.co.za/interviews/april-2017-interviews/jsc-candidates/vijaylutchmee-reddy/.

Wesson, M. & Du Plessis, M. (2008) Fifteen years on: central issues relating to the transformation of the South African judiciary, *South African Journal on Human Rights*, 24, pp. 187–213.

Women in the Nigerian judiciary: considerable headway or organised progress?

Enibokun Uzebu-Imarhiagbe

ABSTRACT

Women have made considerable progress in terms of their entrance into the legal profession, such that they are advancing towards parity with men on the High Court benches in Nigeria. This study is a product of qualitative empirical data gathered from interviews with judges and information gleaned from government records and personal files of judges in the Archives of the judiciaries in Mid-Western Nigeria. It identifies reasons for the increase in the number of women on the High Court Bench in the area. Women entering the legal professions in Nigeria from the 1930s opted for a career in government legal service and the Magistracy with less financial remuneration but regular work hours, than in private legal practice that provides higher remunerations and irregular work hours. Findings reveal that the number of women judges increased when it became fairly established to tunnel 90% of appointments to the High Court from these channels. The preliminary conclusion therefore, is that, although women lawyers have made considerable headway as High Court judges, the increase in their numbers on the High Court bench was not as a result of any organised policy to increase the number of women judges in Nigeria.

Introduction

Within the last two decades, the percentage of women entrants to the Nigerian bar has increased dramatically, so also has women's representation on the High Court bench. While women have made huge strides in the judiciary in some civil law jurisdiction, the same cannot be said of most common law jurisdictions (Boigeol, 2013). The body of international scholarship on women's entry into the courts in common law jurisdictions have tended to focus on explaining why so few women sit on the courts (see for example, Cook, 1989; Palmer, 2001; Schultz & Shaw, 2013). This has in turn created a lacuna, such that the literature addressing women in courts does not take account of peculiar situations where the number of women judges is almost at par with their male colleagues. In Nigeria, women judges are edging towards parity with their male colleagues in the profession. Rather than engaging the question "why so few women serve as judges?" The Nigerian scenario begs the question, "why so many women serve as judges?"

The percentage of women judges serving on the High Court bench in each state in Nigeria varies enormously. However, for the purpose of this paper, the focus is on Midwestern Nigeria, the first region to elevate a woman to a High Court bench. Midwestern Nigeria is used here for the strict purpose of a geographical delimitation of the area which this paper interrogates to refer to the present-day states of Edo and Delta in Nigeria. This paper therefore examines the peculiar context that has made it fertile for women's advancement in the legal profession and thus, the judiciary in Nigeria. Focusing on the period 1963–2010, it argues that evidence from Midwestern Nigeria suggests that the numerical advancement of women in the judiciary was as a result of the career choices they made when they entered the legal profession (Table 1).

This paper is based on extensive qualitative interviews with judges in Mid-Western Nigeria complemented with government records in the High Court archives of Edo and Delta states. In the following discussion, this paper examines the history of the legal profession in Nigeria, it then addresses the factors responsible for the increase in the number of women judges through a discussion of the career trajectories of women in the legal profession in Midwestern Nigeria under the two headings-first, in the judiciary, and second, in the Ministry of Justice. It concludes that the increase in the number of women judges on the High Court bench was gradual and not as a result of a deliberate policy by any particular government to increase the appointment of women judges.

The legal profession: a brief history

The Nigerian legal system is patterned on a Western model. It evolved as a consequence of British colonisation of the area that later became known as Nigeria. The introduction of the British system of courts increased the need for legally trained persons to assist in the administration of justice. Consequently, the Supreme Court Ordinance of 1876[1] empowered the Chief Justice of the Supreme Court to confer the rights to practice law on persons admitted as legal practitioners in the United Kingdom. Western legal structures were then imported as foreign and indigenous lawyers schooled in the laws of the metropole appeared. They became important factors in the reproduction, adaptation and maintenance of Western-inspired legal structure (see, Merry, 1988; Ghai, 1987). The forms and procedures of the superior courts in Nigeria are based

Table 1. Percentage of women judges appointed, 1963–2010[a].

Years	% of women judges
2001–2010	41.3%
1991–2000	35.7%
1981–1990	14.8%
1971–1980	0%
1963–1970	5.9%

[a]"Original". Table and Figure created by the researcher. 2017.

upon those in England. A large part of the statute laws of England have been adapted in Nigeria including the convention of drafting and interpretation, the mode of legal argumentation and procedure as well as the trappings of the wig and the gown.

This seeming dominance of the English common law tradition of Britain in Nigeria obscures the fact that local particularities and realities shaped the development of the legal profession in Nigeria (Adewoye, 1981, p. 53). Unlike the British system, the legal profession in Nigeria is fused; no distinction is maintained between the Barristers and Solicitors. The technical rules of European law and the need to interpret them in the light of the changing circumstances in the Nigerian society, gave rise to the emergence of the "practitioners" of the law, in other words, lawyers (see Adewoye, 1970, p. 101; 1981, p. 53). The implication of this is that the legal profession was not specifically imposed by the colonial administration. Rather, the legal profession was a natural consequence of the European law and the legality that came with colonialism.

The dearth of trained legal practitioners called for people familiar with at least the rudiments of the English legal system. It called into existence a class of men variously referred to as "Local-made Solicitors", "Self-taught Attorneys", "Colonial Solicitors" or simply "Attorneys". They were familiar with the English legal system, but were not qualified lawyers. They dominated the legal profession in Nigeria until about the end of the first decade of the twentieth century (Adewoye, 1969, p. 50). The arrival of qualified lawyers did not automatically drive out the local attorneys. The need of the court exceeded the supply of professionally qualified lawyers. As a result, the Supreme Court continued not only to allow the local attorneys to practise but also to recruit more of their kind until 1913 (Adewoye 1969, p. 57; 1977, p. 34).

It is significant to note that the gender composition of the Bar of local attorneys was exclusively male (Adewoye, 1977, pp. 14–35). This could mean that there was an element of gender prejudice in the colonial administration's attitude towards the selection of women as local attorney. However, this point about gender being a determining factor in the selection of local attorneys in Nigeria should not be pressed too hard. It may just have been possible that women who had the necessary qualifications were simply not available. Furthermore, it was the practice at the time in the United Kingdom that women were not admitted to the Bar and were not allowed to take up paid employment or be involved in public service (Mcglynn, 2003).

The male exclusivity of the legal profession was broken when Stella Jane Thomas was called to the Nigerian Bar in 1935 (Fawehinmi, 1988; Oyeweso, 2014). In Nigeria as in Britain and America, women were latecomers to the legal profession. In many parts of the world, the law profession was still considered an exclusively male profession. In Nigeria, the legal profession was considered a dangerous and masculine job (Solanke, 2007, p. 165). The mobility[2] required of those in private legal practice was very high and rigorous

(Adewoye, 1977, p. 28; Solanke, 2007, p. 165). Many of the first women lawyers in Nigeria had to practice either in their father's or brother's Law Chambers, while others chose a career in government service either in the judiciary as a Magistrate or as a Counsel in the Ministry of Justice (Adewale, 1991, p. 165).

By 1963, when the Midwestern Region was carved out[3] of the Western region (*Constitution of Mid-Western Nigeria Act*, 1964, Section 52), a number of women have been appointed to serve in the lower bench in the Nigerian judiciary. Stella Jane Thomas, the first woman lawyer was also the first woman to be appointed a Magistrate in 1942. Other women who were appointed as Magistrates were Mrs Modupe Eboh (who later became the first woman to be appointed a High Court judge in Nigeria), Mrs Ige (now late Justice Atinuke Ige of the Court of Appeal), Mrs Dulcie Ethel Oguntoye (the first woman to be appointed a Judge of the High Court of Lagos State), and Mrs C. O. Okunuga. A number of these women were eventually elevated to the High Court bench. However, at this time in Nigeria's legal history, there was virtually no woman on the High Court bench in the entire country (See, Federal Republic of Nigeria, 1965. *Staff List As At January, 1965*, pp. 125–126).

Women's career trajectories in the judiciary

The Court plays a pivotal role in the peaceful resolution of disputes. In Nigeria, just like in the United Kingdom and the United States, judges in all courts, from the lower courts of the magistrates up to the Supreme Court are highly regarded. Elevation to a High Court bench is very prestigious and often regarded as the culmination of a successful legal career. There are various hierarchies of courts in Nigeria. At the Apex is the Supreme Court. To be eligible for appointment as a Justice of the Supreme Court, candidates must have practised as a lawyer for not less than fifteen years. Next in the hierarchy of Courts is the Court of Appeal, which is also a federal court. It is exclusively, an appellate court and has exclusive jurisdiction over appeals from all other inferior courts throughout the federation, except appeals from magistrate and customary courts. It is composed of the President of the Court of Appeal and other Justices of the Court of Appeal (*Constitution of the Federal Republic of Nigeria*, 1999, Section 237). A minimum of twelve years post-call experience is required for appointment as a Justice of the Court of Appeal.

Immediately below the Court of Appeal are the High Courts, which exist both at the federal and state government levels. The Federal and the State High Court have equal powers (*Constitution of the Federal Republic of Nigeria*, 1999, Sections, 249, 270 & 273). The High Court of a state is the highest superior court of record in that state. A state's High Court has both unlimited original and appellate jurisdiction with respect to any civil proceeding in which the existence or extent of a legal right, power, duty, liability, privilege, interest, obligation, or claim is at issue (Akande, 1991, p. 63). In addition to its unlimited civil and criminal jurisdiction, the High Court also has original jurisdiction to hear and determine any petition over questions of membership in any legislative house. Each state has its own High Court law, which regulates its practice and procedure. A minimum of ten years post-call experience is required for elevation to the High Court bench. High court judges are recruited from the Bar, the Magistracy, the Ministry of Justice, and more recently, from the Universities. Each state has the power to create and establish any court below the hierarchy of a High Court in terms of both competence and jurisdiction (*Constitution of the Federal Republic of Nigeria*, 1999, Section, 274). Hence, there are magistrate courts, which have original jurisdiction over both civil and criminal proceedings.

There are also customary law courts, namely, the Sharia Court of Appeal and the Customary Court of Appeal, both are appellate courts. The Federal Capital Territory and states with large Islamic populations have the right to establish Sharia Courts of Appeal to administer Islamic civil law. There is a Customary Court of Appeal for the Federal Capital territory and any State that requires it. There also exist District Courts, Area Courts and Customary Courts established in various States by State laws. These courts have limited jurisdiction and appeals to them lie in the High Court, Sharia Courts of Appeal, or Customary Court of Appeal as the case may be (Akande, 1991, p. 63; Abiloro, 2012).[4] Requirement for appointment to the Magistrates courts are professional legal training plus a number of years in practice, ranging from two years in the case of Magistrates Grade III, five years for senior Magistrates and seven years for Chief Magistrates (Oko, 2007, p. 205).

While there were no women on the High Court bench in Midwestern Nigeria until 1969, the 1960s witnessed the entrance of six women into the legal profession in Mid-Western Nigeria. The first woman was Modupe Eboh, a Magistrate in the Western region judiciary. With the excision of the Mid-Western region from the Western region, all officers of Mid-Western origin were asked to transfer their service from the Western region to the Mid-Western region, this included officers married to the Mid-Westerners. This was how Mrs Eboh, a Magistrate in the then Western region who was called to the Nigerian Bar in 1953, transferred her service to Mid-Western Nigeria (Oguntoye, 2008, p. 104).

The second woman was Mrs Lilian Joan Aiwerioghene, a British woman married to a Nigerian. She was called to the Nigerian Bar in 1961 and was appointed a Magistrate in the Judiciary of the region on November 18th, 1963 (Edo State High Court Archives, w.e.f. 18/11/1963, vide PC. 79/1). The third woman was Mrs Olufumilayo Abigail Oni-Okpaku married to a Surgeon, Dr Benji Oni-Okpaku, a Mid-Westerner. She was called to the Nigerian Bar in 1964 and was engaged in private legal practice before taking up appointment on the lower bench in 1969. The forth and the fifth were Mrs M. A. Okungbowa and Miss Constance Momoh, both called to the Nigerian Bar in 1966, and Mrs F. E. Ayanka-Wilson, who was called to the Nigerian

Bar in 1969, was the sixth woman. This was how most of the women called to the bar in the 1950s and 1960s were engaged in serving in the Midwestern region government in both the Ministry of Justice and the Judiciary.

With the elevation of Mrs Modupe Eboh to the High Court bench of the Midwestern Region in 1969 (*Nigerian Official Gazette*, 1969, p. 1834), the region could boast of being the first to appoint a woman to a superior court. On the lower bench, the appointment of Mrs Oni-Okpaku that same year increased the number of women on the Magisterial Bench to two. The High Court Bench was made up of eleven judges, of which one was a woman, and the Lower Bench was made up of twenty-five Magistrates, of which two were women. The 1960s witnessed the appointment of seventeen judges. Out of the seventeen, only one was a woman, accounting for 5.9% of those appointed to the High Court Bench in Midwestern Nigeria in the 1960s (Midwest State Public Service *Staff List*, 1970, pp. 81–82).

When Mrs Modupe Eboh was appointed a High Court judge in 1969, she remained a lone star in the galaxy of the High Court Bench not only in Mid-Western Nigeria, but in the entire Nigeria for the next seven years, until Mrs Dulcie Oguntoye was appointed a judge of Lagos State High Court in 1976. Justice Eboh's appointment placed Nigeria on record as the first country in Africa to elevate a woman to a superior court. When the area was rechristened Bendel State in 1976, there were four women on the lower bench. These women gradually rose through the ranks and were later elevated to the High Court bench.

The opening years of the 1970s witnessed the entrance of more women into the lower bench. However, the number of women in the entire judiciary in the 1970s did not exceed six out of fifty-three judicial officers appointed in that decade (See Bendel State Staff List as at 1st April, 1984). In 1976, Mrs Eboh, transferred her service to the High Court of Lagos State, leaving the High Court Bench in the area devoid of a woman judge. This notwithstanding, there were a number of vacancies in the judiciary. For instance, Magistrate, Grade II position had one vacancy, Senior Magistrate, Grade II and Magistrate, Grade I position had nine vacancies, Senior Magistrate, Grade I position had four vacancies, Chief Magistrates position had seven vacancies, the post of the Chief Registrar was vacant and there was one vacancy for a judge (Bendel State Public Service *Staff List*, 1975, pp. 103–104).

The magistracy has been very unattractive to lawyers in Nigeria because the salaries of magistrates are comparatively low and the working conditions are generally poor. In this early part of the history of the legal profession, and indeed the judiciary in Nigeria, it was generally believed that only a lawyer who has been unsuccessful would take up appointment on the lower bench (Akpata, 1994, pp. 1–2). The unsuccessful lawyer is not necessarily a mediocre, he or she may have a first class brain and possess all the attributes that makes for success at the bar. Yet, success eludes him or her either because he/she is unlucky and does not get good briefs that could project him/her to the limelight, or because he/she has been adhering strictly to the professional ethics of not touting for clients (Fawehinmi, 1988, p. 421). It must be mentioned however, that a lawyer who possesses the trappings of a first class advocate and is capable of having a lucrative practice at the Bar may also opt for the lower bench for the love and dignity of the office (Akpata, 1994, pp. 1–2; Begho, 1988, p. 55).

Also, women lawyers whose fathers or husbands were well placed financially may opt for the lower benches because of the dignity attached to the bench and its regular work hours. Most of the women who took up appointment in the early years of the Judiciary in Mid-Western Nigeria fell into these categories. The implication was that while very few male lawyers took up appointment in the Magistracy, women lawyers were more comfortable there because of the regular work hours. However, at the early period, women remained a minority because the profession has for decades been dominated by men. Unlike their male colleagues, women lawyers were more comfortable taking up appointment as Magistrates on the Lower Bench and as State Counsels in the Ministry of Justice because of the consistent work hours, pay and opportunity for advancement to the High Court (Omorodion, 2012, pp. 77–78; Adekoya, 2009).

On the 17th of March 1976, the Mid-Western region was renamed Bendel State with some minimal boundary adjustments. The judiciary expanded tremendously, especially on the High Court bench. The positions available on the High Court bench, which were usually twelve or fourteen, now increased to twenty-one positions. In 1976, of the twenty-one positions now available for judges, only nineteen were occupied by men leaving two posts vacant (Bendel State Public Service *Staff List*, 1976, p. 107). On the lower bench, no woman was employed that year, their numbers remained the same. Between 1977 and 1979, only two women joined the ranks of the Magistrates (see Bendel State Public Service *Staff List*, 1977–1979).

Women lawyers appointed to the lower bench in the 1960s and early 1970s became eligible for elevation to the High Court Bench and were thus elevated (Bendel State Public Service, 1980, pp. 115–116). By 1979, virtually all the women that were elevated to the High Court bench in the 1980s had reached the peak of their career on the lower bench. For instance, Mrs Aiwerioghene who was elevated to the High Court bench in 1982, was already a Chief Magistrate in 1971, she had to wait another eleven years before being elevated, becoming the first woman to be elevated to the position of a judge in Bendel State. Information gathered from the field reveal that Mrs Aiwerioghene was not discriminated against based on gender, but rather, based on her nationality.[5] She was a white British woman that insisted on retaining her British citizenship status.

Mrs Oni-Okpaku, the second woman to be so elevated in 1985, was already a Chief Magistrate in 1980. Mrs Okungbowa, the third woman to be appointed a judge in 1988, was already a Chief Magistrate by 1979. While Mrs Omorodion, the fourth and last woman to be appointed a judge before the area was divided into Edo and Delta States, became a Chief Magistrate in 1983 and a Solicitor-General and Permanent Secretary, Ministry of Justice in 1988 before her elevation in 1990. The elevation of these women were not token, they had gathered the requisite experience and were amply qualified for elevation to the High Court bench. Between 1981 and 1991, twenty-eight Judges were appointed to the High Court bench. Only four these were women, accounting for 14.3% of the total number of judges appointed in those years. Indeed, when compared with the earlier periods, that is, 5.9% in the 1960s and 0% in the 1970s, women had made considerable progress on the High Court bench in Mid-Western Nigeria.

By 1990, it is interesting to note that at the junior and entry levels of the Magistracy, from the ranks of Magistrates Grade I down to the ranks of Magistrates Grade III the number of women now exceeded those of the men, buttressing the point made earlier that the magistracy was unattractive to male lawyers. In the Magistrates Grade I posts, of the twelve posts available, only four were occupied leaving eight vacancies, two of those posts were occupied by women. There existed on the Magistrates Grade II and Magistrates Grade III ranks 35 posts, only eleven posts out of these were occupied leaving twenty-four vacancies. Women accounted for six out of the eleven posts occupied (Bendel State Public Service *Staff List*, 1988, p. 115). The foundation was set for the increased visibility of women in the judiciary, as most of these women were later elevated to the High Court bench.

Although, by 1991, women judges were still a minority, they had inadvertently registered their presence on the High Court bench in Mid-Western Nigeria. Women represented only 7.7% of the total number of judges appointed from 1963 to 1991. Nonetheless, they were gradually making inroads into a profession that had hitherto been dominated by men. When the area was divided into Edo and Delta States on the 27th of August 1991, judges who were indigenes of the newly carved out Delta state had to transfer their services to the Judiciary of the newly created state to ease its smooth take off. The judges who relocated and became pioneer judges of Delta state were fifteen and only one woman was among their rank.

Three new judges were appointed to complement the efforts of the pioneer judges of the newly created states, another woman was appointed thus, increasing the number of women in the Delta State Judiciary to two. In Edo state, those who remained excluding those that had retired were twenty-two. Two new judges were appointed in 1991 bringing the number of the judges in the State to twenty-four. Thus, the number of women judges in both Edo and Delta states at their inception in 1991 were, two and three respectively. With the appointment of Constance Momoh as a judge in 1992, the total number of women on the bench in Edo State increased to four (High Court Archives,

Edo State, Confidential Files of Judges). As the judiciary of both states continued to expand, more women judges were appointed.

Within the next ten years, that is between the year 2000 and 2010, about forty-five judges were appointed in the judiciary of the states in the area.[6] The number of women judges appointed were twenty-one, accounting for 41.3% of the total number of judges. It is evident that by 2010 there had been a significant penetration of women into all the ranks of the judiciary in Mid-Western Nigeria. The area has produced four women Chief Judges and a President of the Customary Court of Appeal, two from each state respectively. If not for the fact that Hon Justice Omorodion was lost to the cold hands of death few months before her appointment as the Chief Judge of Edo State, the area would have produced five women Chief Judges by 2010.

Women's career trajectories in the Ministry of Justice

Lawyers in the Ministry of Justice are responsible for the legal needs of government, government ministries and agencies. Although lawyers are posted to other ministries to handle the legal work of such Ministries, they remain the employees of the Ministry of Justice. According to Oko (2007) approximately seventy-five percent of lawyers in government service entered the civil service directly after their National Youth Service Corp (NYSC),[7] while others had a brief stint in private practice before accepting government employment. Rank at the time of appointment depends upon experience. Lawyers who just completed their NYSC assignment were employed as Pupil State Counsels, then they advanced to senior positions, the highest being a director in any of the departments within the Ministry.

Movement from one position to another ordinarily takes an average of three years. However, factors such as performance, political connections and availability of a vacancy may affect the rate of promotion. In some cases, top officials in the Ministry of Justice have been appointed as judges of federal and state High Courts. Data on lawyers in the Ministry of Justice indicates that government lawyers have been considered favourably for judicial appointments. In the early part of the history of the judiciary, it appears that in appointing judges, the practicing Bar has been given preference over the Magistracy (Oko, 2007, pp. 202–204).

Mrs Eboh was the first woman to be employed in the Ministry of Justice. She rose to the highest promotional position in the Ministry, the position of the Director of Public Prosecution in 1967 and served in acting capacity as Solicitor-General and Permanent Secretary before her elevation to the High Court bench in 1969. After her elevation, the Ministry of Justice was devoid of a woman legal practitioner until 1973 when Miss M. T. Okorodudu was appointed as a Pupil State Counsel (see Midwest State Public Service *Staff List*, 1974, p. 76). By the time the area was renamed Bendel State in 1976, there were just four women lawyers amongst the seventeen lawyers in the entry positions of State Counsel Grade II and Pupil State Counsel in the Ministry of Justice. However, there were ample vacancies for those who were qualified regardless of gender (Bendel State Public Service *Staff List*, 1975, pp. 79–80).

Women lawyers who were employed within the first five years of the 1970s started moving up and were fast closing ranks with their male colleagues. Some of these women lawyers rose to the post of Senior State Counsel Grade I and were in a majority at that level.

The post of State Counsel Grade II and Pupil State Counsel had twenty-one posts available, of the twenty-one posts, six posts were occupied. Women occupied three out of the four posts at State Counsel Grade 1 level and three out of the six posts at the State Counsel Grade II and Pupil State Counsel ranks. In spite of this, women lawyers were still a minority in the Ministry considering the fact that they were just six out of the total number of 39 lawyers in the ministry (Bendel State Public Service *Staff List*, 1975, p. 79).

From 1984 onwards, women lawyers were a majority in all the mid-level posts in the Ministry of Justice. For instance, in 1983, Mrs T. A. Wilson was the only Principal State Counsel Grade II occupying one out of the eight positions available. The rank of Senior State Counsel Grade I had twenty-two vacancies, women accounted for three out of the five positions occupied. The same scenario existed at the level of Senior State Counsel Grade II. Out of the twenty-eight positions available, only five posts were occupied, leaving twenty-three vacancies, three out of those positions were occupied by women (Bendel State Public Service *Staff List*, 1984, pp. 149–150).

Of the three lawyers that were in Principal State Counsel Grade II level in the Ministry of Justice, two were women. While at Senior State Counsel Grade I level, women accounted for five out of the eight lawyers in that grade by 1985 (Bendel State Public Service *Staff List*, 1986, pp. 104–105). In 1986, women accounted for two out of the four lawyers in the rank of Principal State Counsel Grade I position and were the only two lawyers in the Principal State Counsel Grade II positions. At Senior State Counsel Grade I level, women accounted for three out of the four lawyers there, while at the Senior State Counsel Grade II level, women numbered three out of the six lawyers in that grade (Bendel State Public Service *Staff List*, 1987, p. 101). In 1988, Mrs J. O. Omorodion was appointed to head the Ministry of Justice as the Solicitor-General and Permanent Secretary, making her the second woman in Mid-Western Nigeria to occupy that position. She was still occupying that position when she was appointed a High Court Judge in 1990 (Bendel State Public Service *Staff List*, 1988, p. 90).

By 1990, about fifty women lawyers had passed through the Judiciary and the Ministry of Justice. Mid-Western Nigeria had witnessed the entrance of about seventy-seven women into the legal profession. When compared with their male colleagues, they were still a minority in the profession. However, it is interesting to note that these women lawyers were relatively young in comparison with their male colleagues. For example, in the Ministry of justice, T. A. Wilson, (Mrs) who came into the profession in 1976 was born in 1950, compared with her bosses who were male and were all born in the 1930s. This same scenario existed in the judiciary too (See Bendel State Public Service *Staff List*, 1984, pp. 149–150).

The implication is that when it became fairly established to tunnel judges from the Ministry of Justice and the Magistracy, their male colleagues had reached the compulsory retirement age of sixty-five and left service. While the women who were just entering the legal profession who favoured a career in government service, had risen to top positions, becoming eligible for appointment as High Court judges.

Conclusion

A survey of women's career trajectories in the legal professions in Nigeria is attempted in an effort to explain the increasing visibility of Women judges in Nigeria. What is discernible from the above account is that the history of women in the legal profession is not a history of exclusion but of reception and advancement. In the admission and appointment of women lawyers into the bar and the bench, there was no deliberate consensus or policy by government to achieve gender integration. The driving force was need, the need for qualified legal practitioners. The judiciary and the Ministry of justice constantly had vacancies that needed to be filled. The implication of these vacancies was that there was enough room for the absorption of qualified candidates regardless of gender. The demand for lawyers exceeded the number of those enrolled into the profession at this time. There continued to be vacancies for qualified legal practitioners in the Ministry of Justice and the Judiciary throughout the 1970s and 1980s.

While the majority of male lawyers opted for private practice because it was more lucrative to be in private legal practice, than in government service, women found it attractive because of its regular work hours and reduced mobility. As a result, most young male lawyers did not look to the lower bench or the entry level positions in the Ministry of Justice for a career in the legal profession. Nonetheless, since most of those enrolling to the Nigerian Bar at this time were men, the few that took up appointment in the Ministry of Justice and the judiciary initially surpassed the number of women. The point is that the paucity of women judges from the 1960 down to the 1990 was not peculiar to Mid-western Nigeria; it was largely a consequence of the low enrolment rate of women in the legal profession in Nigeria within the first three decades after independence. As women entered the profession, they opted for a career in government service either in the Magistracy or in the Ministry of Justice. When it became fairly established to tunnel judges from these channels, the majority of senior lawyers were women. This to a large extent explains the increased visibility of women in the judiciary in Nigeria in recent years.

Although an adaptation of the Western model, the legal profession in Nigeria did not follow the trajectories of the Western model, whereby women were discriminated and initially excluded from the profession. Thus, women were able to penetrate almost all aspects of the legal profession in Nigeria within a relatively short period after their entrance. This is traceable to local particularities that have shaped the profession from the era of when "unlearned" judges and locally-made solicitors had to operate the judicial machinery. This impacted on women's entry into the judiciary in Nigeria. Due to shortage of qualified lawyers willing to work in government service, women lawyers were employed in those aspects of government service that required a qualified lawyer, such as the Justice Department and the Judiciary. Many women lawyers entering the legal profession in Nigeria found their way into the lower bench and from there, to the High Court Bench. The acceptance of women into the legal profession in Nigeria, like the employment of self-taught attorneys was essentially a result of adaptation to circumstances.

However, as you go higher in the hierarchy of the Courts in Nigeria, this visibility of women judges is not readily apparent. This notwithstanding, women judges have attained parity and even numerically surpassed their male colleague, and in recent times, within a relatively short period of time after their enrolment at the Bar in State Judiciaries. In spite of this, women judges in Nigeria continue to face peculiar challenges and obstacles, especially with regards to appointment into the Federal High Courts, the Court of Appeal and even the Supreme Court. Their number in the Federal judiciaries is limited, especially, in Court of Appeal and the Supreme Court. This is largely due to the fact that in a relatively complex society like Nigeria, judges are appointed into Federal Courts, even the Supreme Court, not on merit but on grounds of Federal character, geo-political entity, religious and ethnic balancing which ironically in the past tends to favour only men in the profession.

The appointment of the first female Supreme Court Justice in 2005 which culminated in her rising to the position of Chief Justice of Nigeria in 2012 marked the beginning of a new era for women judges in Nigeria. Women judges can now hope to attain their dreams of becoming Justices of the apex court in Nigeria. More women are now been appointed into the Supreme Court Bench without requiring a longer waiting time than their male colleagues. Although, their numbers are still few in comparison with their male colleagues, progress is been made and the number women judges at all levels of the judiciary in Nigeria keeps growing.

Notes

1. As soon as the British formally established a colony in Lagos in 1861, they found it necessary to introduce the English law and legal institutions for the purpose of administering the colony. This led to the establishment of various types of courts in Nigeria. (For more information about the introduction of British system of courts in Nigeria, see Adewoye, 1969, pp. 51–52; 1970).

2. Up to 1886, the British West African colonies were not regarded as separate entities in official circles. Lagos was, at first, part of the General Administration centred in Sierra Leone and later on, from 1874, it was administered as part of the Gold Coast Colony. The professional activities of lawyers spread beyond the colony of Lagos, to these areas.
3. Initially, the area was part of the Western Region until it was excised and made an independent region, see Vickers (2000).
4. Nigeria has a pluralistic legal system with common law, customary law and Islamic law as the major legal traditions in the country. Appeals from the lower Customary courts and lower Sharia courts lay in the High Court, the Customary Court of Appeal or in the Sharia Court of Appeal.
5. Interviews conducted with Hon Justice Omage (Rtd), Benin City, 29/05/2017 and Bar P. D. Agidigbi, Benin City, 14/06/2017. Also, it was the case in Nigeria at the time that without Nigerian citizenship, one had no professional future in the Public Service (Oguntoye, 2008, p. 99). The constitution made provisions for aliens married to Nigerians to acquire Nigerian citizenship after meeting certain requirements one of which was the renunciation of previous citizenship status (The Constitution of the Federal Republic of Nigeria, 1960, Chapter 11, Section 8, Sub-section 2–3; The Nigerian Citizenship Act of 1960; for an explanation of conditions see Okoli, 1990, pp. 27–28).
6. Gleaned from the Public Service *Staff List* in Delta & Edo State High Court Archives.
7. Women also participated in the National Youth Service Corp (NYSC) under which graduates of universities and polytechnics were required to undergo a compulsory one year national service outside their state of origin was established in 1973 to foster national integration. The scheme, which is still operative, is meant to transcend political, social, state and ethnic loyalties.

Disclosure statement

No potential conflict of interest was reported by the author(s).

References

Abiloro, S.O. (2012) Jurisdiction and courts established by the constitution, Being a Paper Presented at the *'Legal Intervention and Procedures in Environmental Health Litigation' Conference, Ta'al Hotel, Lafia*, 18–20th.

Adekoya, F. (2009) The changing phases of the legal profession and the impact of gender and diversity in Nigeria. Available at: https:/www.ibanet.org, accessed 12 November 2015.

Adewale, T. (1991) *Reminiscence at the Bar* (Ibadan, Bookcraft Ltd).

Adewoye, O. (1969) Self-taught attorneys in Lagos, 1865–1913, *Journal of the Historical Society of Nigeria*, 5(1), pp. 47–65.

Adewọye, O. (1970) Prelude to the legal profession in Lagos 1861–1880, *Journal of African Law*, 14(2), pp. 98–114.

Adewoye, O. (1977) *The judicial system of Southern Nigeria 1854–1954: Law and justice in a dependency* (New Jersey, Humanities Press).

Adewọye, O. (1981) Legal practice in Ibadan, 1904–1960, *Journal of the Historical Society of Nigeria*, 11(1), pp. 52–66.

Akande, J. (1991) The legal order and the administration of federal and state courts, *Publius, Federalism in Nigeria: Toward Federal Democracy*, 21(4), pp. 61–73.

Akpata, E. (1994) *Justice for All and by All* (Lagos, B & C Publishers Limited).

Aluyi, I. (2016) *Interview* (Retired Judge).

Begho, M.A. (1988) *The Dogbite Magistrate His Struggles (An Autobiography)* (Lagos, Daily Times).

Bendel State Public Service. *Staff List*, 1975–1988 (Benin City, Ministry of Establishments).

Boigeol, A. (2013) Feminisation of the French magistrature: gender and judging in a feminised context, in: U. Schultz & G. Shaw (Eds) *Gender and Judging* (Oxford: Hart Publishing), pp. 125–144.

Constitution of Mid-Western Nigeria Act. (1964).

Cook, B.B. (1989) Women judges in the opportunity structure, in: L.L. Crites & Hepperle (Eds) *Women, Courts and Equality* (London, Sage Publications), pp. 143–174.

Eborieme, V. (2016) *Interview* (Judge).

Ehighiamusoe, A. (2016) *Interview* (Judge).

Epstein, C. (1981) *Women in Law* (New York, Basic Books).

Fawehinmi, G. (1988) *Bench and Bar* (Lagos, Nigerian Law Publications Ltd).

Federal Republic of Nigeria (1965) *Staff List As At January, 1965* (Lagos, Federal Ministry of Establishment).

Ghai, Y. (1987) Law, development and African scholarship, *The Modern Law Review*, 50(6), pp. 750–776.

High Court Archives, Delta State, Staff Confidential Files; High Court Archives, Edo State, Confidential Files of Judges, personnel archives.

Ikponmwen, F. (2016) *Interview* (Judge).

Mcglynn, C. (2003) The status of women lawyers in the United Kingdom, in: U. Schultz & G. Shaw (Eds) *Women in the World's Legal Professions* (Oregon, Hart Publishing).

Merry, S.E. (1988) Legal Pluralism, *Law & Society Review*, 22(5), pp. 869–896.

Midwest State Public Service. (1969–1974) *Staff List* (Benin City, Ministry of Establishments).

Oguntoye, A. (2008) *Your Estranged Faces* (Maryland, USA, Pinnacle Publications).

Okoli, K.C. (1990) Nigerian citizenship law: A current perspective, *Journal of African Law*, 34 (1), pp. 27–41.

Oko, O. (2007) *Problems and Challenges for Lawyers in Africa, Lessons from Nigeria* (UK, The Edwin Mellen Press, Ltd).

Omage, V.A.O. (2017) *Interview* (Retired Judge).

Omoregie, E. (2016) *Interview* (Lawyer).

Omorodion, A.A. (2012). *I Will Not Let God Down: The Life and Times of a Princess* (Benin City: Habiba Balogun Consulting).

Oni-Okpaku, A. (2017) *Interview* (Retired Judge).

Oyeweso, S. (2014) Breaking the yoke of patriarchy: Nigerian women in the various professions, politics and governance, 1914–2014. Lecture Delivered at the 2014 National Conference of Association of Women Judges of Nigeria (NAWJN).

Palmer, B. (2001) 'To do justly', the integration of women into the American judiciary, *Political Science and Politics*, 34(2), pp. 235–239.

Schultz, U. & Shaw, G. (Eds) (2013) *Gender and Judging* (Oxford: Hart Publishing).

Solanke, F. (2007) *Reaching for the Stars: The Autobiography of 'Folake Solanke'* (Ibadan, Book-Builders)

Supreme Court Ordinance. (1876).

The Constitution of the Federal Republic of Nigeria. (1999).

Ukhuegbe, S. (2016) *Interview* (Lawyer).

Vickers, M. (2000) *Ethnicity and Sub-Nationalism in Nigeria: Movement for a Mid-West State* (Oxford, UK: World View Publishing).

The glass ceiling at the highest levels of the Spanish judiciary

Mónica García Goldar

ABSTRACT
In Spain, the number of female judges at the highest levels of the judiciary is very low, despite the approval of two Strategic Plans for Equality in the Judicial Career (2013 and 2020). This situation does not seem to differ from other European countries, according to the data offered by CEPEJ (2018). It is clear that the end of tokenism has not yet arrived, and for that reason, an analysis of the main probable causes for this glass ceiling is carried out in this paper. A greater effort must be made in order to overcome this situation and achieve a better representation of female judges at the highest levels of the judiciary system.

Introduction

The low presence of female judges at the highest levels of the Spanish judiciary system is a real cause for concern. Apart from the Labour Chamber, where there are 5 female judges out of 13 (38%), in the Administrative Chamber there are 4 female judges out of 33 (12%), and in the rest of Chambers of the Supreme Court there is only one female judge out of 10 (Civil Chamber, 10%) or 12 (Criminal and Military Chamber, 8%). These numbers get even lower when we look at the Government Committee of the Spanish Supreme Court where there are no female judges at all.

This glass ceiling situation seems to have become sadly permanent. In September 2019, a vacancy at the Civil Chamber of the Supreme Court was advertised and, despite the fact that one of the female applicants seemed to be objectively better suited to the position, a male candidate was eventually selected for the role. This led to a campaign of protest by lawyers and the press to denounce this decision.[1] It is worth noting that the appointment of judges for the Spanish Supreme Court is discretional and corresponds to the General Board of the Judiciary, a traditionally male-dominated body (until 1985 there was no female member at all) that has recently achieved a reasonable parity: nine members out of twenty-one are women.

In the Spanish Constitutional Court, the highest decision-making body for matters such as fundamental rights, there are only two female judges out of twelve (17%). The first female judge in this Court was Gloria Begué (1981–

1989). Between 1989–1998 there were no female judges at all and between 1998 and 2011, there were just 3 female judges: Elisa Pérez Vega, Adela Asúa Batarrita and María Emilia Casas Bahamonde, who also became the first female President of the Constitutional Court. Since 2012, there have only been two female judges: María Encarnación Roca Trías and María Luisa Balaguer Callejón (since 2017). In this case, it is even more difficult to understand the low presence of female judges, because according to the article 159 of the Spanish Constitution, the Constitutional Court is composed of 12 members: 4 are proposed by the Congress; 4 are proposed by the Senate; 2 are proposed by the Government, and 2 are proposed by the General Board of the Judiciary. That is, practically all the appointments are proposed by the Legislative and the Executive power, and this seems contradictory: the institutions that have proposed and passed the Spanish Equality Act 2007, whose main purpose is to implement certain "positive actions" and "try to rebalance pre-existing discriminatory situations", are the first ones not to act in accordance with its spirit.

In 2012, a section of the General Board of the Judiciary (the Equality Commission) was created, which developed the Strategic Plan for Equality in the Judicial Career (2013). This plan contained a series of measures to be adopted in order to achieve "effective equality" in eleven areas of action: access to judicial career, career advancement within the judiciary, vocational training and awareness-raising, family and work conciliation, occupational health and safety, non-sexist language, remuneration, inspection procedure, international relations, new technologies, information and participation. Regrettably, the situation has not changed much since then and this is why the Spanish media has recently shown its concern about this evident glass ceiling at the judiciary.[2] The II Strategic Plan for Equality in the Judicial Career (2020) has been approved very recently, and considers a series of measures in twenty different areas of action. In addition to the eleven previously considered areas, the plan also considers: territorial stability, harassment and violence, age management, equality networks, equality cross-cutting, judging with a gender perspective, annual report, monitoring, review and execution of the Equality plan. This current Strategic Plan analyzes the changes seen over the last few years and states that although there has been progress, it is insufficient.

This glass ceiling is not only visible in Spain. According to a study carried out by CEPEJ (European Commission for the Efficiency of Justice) with data from 2016, it is clear that the percentage of female judges in some European countries is, in general, still very low at the highest levels of the judiciary, although there are many differences between countries (and also in the way judges are selected, especially between civil and common law countries). Specifically, in respect of the National Supreme Courts, the country with the lowest number of female judges is Luxembourg, with a worrying 0%, followed by Albania (9%) and Spain (12%). The country with the highest number of women judges in the Supreme Court is Romania, with 83%.

It is worth mentioning the three patterns of female presence in courts that can be found, described by Cook (1978): the ladder, the pyramid and the bell pattern. Cook's ladder pattern involves equal access by court level, the pyramid pattern describes greater access to lower than higher courts, and the inverted bell pattern shows token access at the top and bottom but not at the major trial level. The ladder pattern can be found in Armenia, where the percentages of female judges in the courts are almost the same (25% female judges in 1st instance courts, 24% female judges in 2nd instance courts, and 29% female judges in national Supreme Court). The bell inverted pattern can be found in Ireland: 36% female judges in 1st instance courts, 20% female judges in 2nd instance courts and 44% female judges in the Supreme Court. Lastly, the pyramid pattern can be found when analysing the average of all countries: 57% female judges in 1st instance courts, 50% female judges in 2nd instance courts, and 37% female judges in national Supreme Courts. The vast majority of countries follow this pattern, including Spain (60% – 37% – 12%). In some of them (France, Greece, Hungary, Latvia, Slovakia and Slovenia) the presence of women judges has already reached or exceeds parity in the highest courts (more than 40%), despite the fact that the number of female judges decreases.

In addition to these three models described by Blair Cook, one could add two more: the balloon pattern and the inverted pyramid pattern. The balloon pattern shows a greater female presence at the appeal courts than 1st instance courts or the Supreme Court. This pattern can be found, for example, in Sweden (49% female judges in 1st instance courts, 58% in 2nd instance courts and 33% in the Supreme Court). The inverted pyramid pattern shows greater access to the higher courts, and can be found in Romania (72% female judges in 1st instance courts, 74% female judges in 2nd instance courts, and 83% female judges in national Supreme Court).

It is clear that, with some exceptions, there is a glass ceiling in the Spanish and other European judiciaries. In this paper I aim to describe the evolution of the presence of women in the Spanish judiciary and also suggest some of the possible causes for this glass ceiling, i.e. sex discrimination and the difficulty in reconciling family life and work. It is this writer's opinion that the ultimate objective is not reaching a complete and absolute *feminization* of the judiciary, but rather reaching parity between male and female judges. A first step would be to achieve an improved female representation rate at all stages of the judiciary between 40% and 60%; the percentage range that is ideal for reaching parity and equality according to the European Commission and its publication *One hundred words for equality* (1998).

The importance of reaching parity at the judiciary

The entry of women into the public life was not straight forward. The struggles fought in the last century, such as those over the right to vote or the right to education, highlighted the unjustifiable worldwide inequality faced by the female population. The feminist movement won battles little by little and there are still many other battles to be won. In this sense, it is worth noting that many countries still remember their pioneering women. Some of the stories surrounding these pioneer women read like an inverted version of Billy Wilder's film *Some Like It Hot* (1959) although without the humour. This is the case in the story of Concepción Arenal, a woman born in Ferrol (Spain, 1820) who had to cut her hair and dress as a man in order to be able to study law at the Central University of Madrid.

Even when it was possible for women to have access to an equal education, access to studying law was not automatic and there were other obstacles for women wishing to practice law. International authors have always historically referred to Law as a male-dominated field (Cook, 1978; Rhode, 1987; Connelly & Hilliard, 1993; Forell & Matthews, 2000).

In Spain, one of the oldest normative bodies, *Las Siete Partidas* (13th century, in force until the nineteenth century) expressly forbade women practicing the profession of law and, tacitly, the profession of judges (Otero Parga, 2013). Many centuries later, during the second Spanish Republic (1931–1936), the Spanish Constitution of 1931 was approved, the fundamental milestone of which was to recognise the right to vote for women (Collado Mateo, 2006). All discrimination based on sex was formally prohibited; however, difficulties faced by women attempting to access the judiciary and the prosecution remained. The Minister of Justice, through the Order of November 16, 1934, denied women's access to the prosecution, the judiciary and the judicial secretariat, arguing that the exercise of these functions required conditions that education and nature gave only to men. The end of the Spanish Civil War (1936–1939) meant the yearning for legal equality that had arisen for women during the Republican period and one of the first repressive measures from the Francoist regime was to suspend the exercise of the few women who had entered the practice of law: Victoria Kent, Clara Campoamor and María Luisa Algarra (Sánchez González, 2012).

Access to the judiciary was denied to women in Spain until 1966, when a limitation established in article 3.2.(c) of the 1961 Act on Women's Rights was removed. This Act contained one simple article which came to remedy the historical error that prevented women from accessing the administration of justice; a historical error that was a consequence of the society at that time. This Act was important, not only because it changed women's rights, but also because it explained why:

> the reasons for the protection that the Law wanted to dispense to the feelings of women must be estimated overcome by the social reality itself and because women who want to exercise the judicial function will satisfy their vocation, which will compensate them for the afflictions that may come their way.

The first woman to become judge was Concepción Carmen Venero in 1971, five years after the Act was passed, but her work was limited to the family law field.[3] It was not until in 1978 – when the last and currently-in-force Spanish Constitution was approved – that Josefina Triguero became the first Spanish female judge as we understand it today: a first instance female judge (Sánchez González, 2012). In 1984, Spain signed and ratified the Convention on the Elimination of All Forms of Discrimination against Women (CEDAW), adopted by the United Nations in 1979. In 2007, the above-mentioned Equality Act was passed, which had a huge impact, compelling all the public and private structures to promote the participation of women and to effectively integrate the principle of equality in all spheres (Novo Canto, 2014).

In recent decades, the number of female judges has not stopped growing. In fact, in 2018, 70% of people who passed the judiciary examinations were women.[4] For that reason, Gómez Bahillo *et al.*, (2016) considered that the feminisation of the Spanish justice system was now a reality. However, the high presence of female judges is only seen at the lowest levels of the Spanish judiciary.

It is important to reach parity at the highest levels of the judiciary and there are many arguments to support this. One reason is that researchers have assumed women judges are more likely to be feminist; accordingly, if we want to promote women's rights, we should promote women judges (Kenney, 2013). The European study "Mapping the representation of women and men in legal professions across the EU" (2017) cites at least three others reasons: firstly, it promotes the "equity principle". The underlying idea is that it is inherently unfair if men have a near monopoly of judicial power and since one of the primary functions of the judiciary is to promote equality and fairness, it would be incompatible if the very instrument charged with that goal should itself exclude women from its ranks. The second reason relates to the concept of democratic legitimacy. A judiciary that operates in a diverse society must itself be diverse in order to better understand and respond to diverse social and individual contexts and experiences. As Maule (2000) states, "a court system that does not reflect the membership of society breeds increasingly higher levels of disaffection and disillusionment. Thus, as more women are placed on the bench, the democratic regime is strengthened". Thirdly, women can make a difference and this may be the most important argument. American doctrine has studied this question extensively, especially after Carol Gilligan's study (1982): *A different voice: Psychological Theory and Womens Development*, which many authors have echoed (Wilson, 1990; Arbour, 1993; Coontz, 2000; Fix and Johnson, 2017) or contested (see *Gender and Judging*, 2013). According to Gilligan, men and women resolve problems in very different ways, and women are more likely to express an ethic of care reflecting values such as empathy, communication and connectedness. This study has inspired feminist scholars to defend the need for a greater gender perspective and to argue for the increased presence of women in the judiciary (Wilson, 1990), because the inclusion of female judges could promote the substantive representation of women's interests in society and create a court more receptive to the concerns of women (Fix & Johnson, 2017). As Wilson argues (1990),

> if women lawyers and women judges through their differing perspectives on life can bring a new humanity to bear on the decision-making process, perhaps they will make a difference. Perhaps they will succeed in infusing the law with an understanding of what it means to be fully human.

Authors have not reached unanimity with regard to whether or not female judges offer a different voice[5], and it is arguably too early to comprehensively analyse this question as the number of female judges in higher courts is still so small that it does not allow for empirical studies (Arbour, 1993). However, reaching parity within the judiciary is, as previously stated, very important. And for that reason, we should reflect on the Spanish glass ceiling and its possible causes.

The glass ceiling in the Spanish judiciary and its possible causes

It has been said that the underrepresentation of female judges in the Spanish Supreme Court is due to the fact that it is only quite recently that they have been allowed to access judicial careers. I do not consider this to be a sufficient explanation, for two main reasons: first, women have been part of the judiciary for 50 years. According to Gómez Bahillo, Elboj Saso and Marcén Muñío (2016), in 2014, there were 614 female judges and magistrates between 51 and 60 years of age, and 73 between 61 and 70 years of age, many of whom complied with the conditions to be in charge of high responsibility positions. Second, it is not necessary to be judge in order to be proposed for the Supreme Court. According to article 345 of the Judiciary Act, lawyers and prestigious jurists may be appointed *Magistrados* (judges) of the Supreme Court if they meet all the requirements established by the General Board of the Judiciary and have carried out their professional activity for a period of more than fifteen years. Taking into account the reduced number of positions at the Spanish Supreme Court, it is hard to believe that there are not enough qualified female judges to be nominated. I believe that the real causes are different: firstly, discrimination on grounds of sex, secondly, the difficulties for female judges in reconciling family and work life.

Sex discrimination

In relation to the Spanish judiciary, Ammerman Yebra (2017) has shown that some women do not get access to high positions in the judiciary due to sex discrimination. This author mentions some cases ruled by the Spanish Supreme Court that make this clear.

The first case is related to two Supreme Court rulings, dated March 9 and 10, 2017. In this case, two candidates –a female and a male candidate–, applied for a promotion to the presidency of an appeal court (second instance) and eventually the male candidate was chosen. The female candidate filed two appeals, one within the procedure of violation of fundamental rights and another ordinary procedure alleging, among other things, sex discrimination. Both appeals were dismissed by the Civil Chamber of the Supreme Court, in which there were no female judges at that moment. Only one judge voted against the final decision: Sieira Míguez. This judge considered that the female candidate had more merits than the male candidate for the position because she was more than one hundred positions ahead of the male candidate in the ranks of the Judicial Career and because she also had more experience in collegiate bodies than the male candidate and therefore the principle of non-discrimination based on sex was being violated.

The second case commented on by Ammerman Yebra is the Spanish Supreme Court decision of June 27, 2017. In this case, again two candidates (female and male) applied for a promotion, this time to the presidency of a regional superior court (*Tribunal Superior de Justicia*). Once again, the male candidate was chosen, without any detailed justification. Due to the lack of justification the Supreme Court ruled to annul this appointment and forced the General Board of the Judiciary to justify their selection. Fifteen days later, the General Board of the Judiciary reached another agreement to appoint the male candidate, arguing that his profile was better for the challenges of the judicial organisation. It is worth noting that there were five votes against this agreement, that is, five members of the General Board of the Judiciary out of thirteen considered that the female candidate had a better profile, and that as women are absolutely underrepresented in these positions she should have been considered for the promotion. They considered that the Equality Act is only an adornment, so "we can –they said– prepare its obituary, because if this guiding principle is not applied in a case as clear as this one, it is because the majority has decided that it will never be applied". The female candidate filed an appeal against this decision but in the end the Spanish Supreme Court dismissed the appeal stating that the General Board of the Judiciary has a broad discretional power when prioritising merits and capabilities of candidates. In addition, there were some judges who voted against the final decision.

It is important to find out why these two women, and surely others, are discriminated against at the highest levels of the judiciary, when the appointments are made discretionally (Gómez Bahillo *et al.*, 2016). In my opinion, there are two plausible explanations.

The first explanation is that men in power (in this case, men in the General Board of the Judiciary) want to preserve their privileges. Valpuesta (2016) wrote, referring to the political class, yet applicable to the judiciary, that men find themselves in a privileged situation that would be seriously threatened if the incorporation of women into political life were a reality. To avoid this, the male power circuits are preserved with the complicity of their peers.

The second explanation for this sex discrimination is due to stereotypes. Collado Mateo (2006) says that it is often argued, when women claim their rights, that there is no longer in the Spanish legal system a single precept that limits them; however, neither the Constitution nor the laws, by themselves, change behaviour, although they may account for the social changes that are taking place. In her opinion, it is difficult to fight against gender stereotypes and historical structures of discrimination based on the supposed inferior nature of women and their "natural" link to the private-domestic space and to the upbringing and care of children.

Stereotypes also force women to prove their competence over and over again. An example is the so called "double bind dilemma": a study from Catalyst (2007) showed that women are seen too soft or too tough, but never just right; that female leaders face higher standards and lower rewards than men leaders; and that female leaders are perceived as competent or likeable, but rarely both. It is also said in this study that the impact of stereotypical bias is often underestimated, because stereotypes create an invisible barrier to women's advancement that is difficult to combat or even detect.

Lorente Acosta (2014) believes that motherhood stereotypes are a "cultural trap". Starting from the biological point of view something artificial has been built: the whole identity of women around motherhood. Acosta argues that motherhood is a transcendent and vital issue, but not to the point that women's entire identity depends on it. And once this identity is built, it is normalised and presented as "the natural" identity. Women are conceived to be mothers and to take care of others: this is the cultural conception. So women can either behave as they are expected to or they will be considered bad women or misguided women. The "culture trap" means that the achievements they obtain are seen as a loss of the traditional role. In the end, they are no longer identified as women or men, with the feminine or the masculine. This is because masculinity continues to be the dominant reference, and femininity continues to be its complement. So it has been throughout history and across the entire planet: there has been no culture in which this model, with different variations, has not been reproduced. Spanish culture, which has been patriarchal and androcentric for so long, has stereotyped men and women. Men are the stronger sex, while women are the weaker sex. So women are believed, even by themselves, not to fit for leadership positions. Wald (2013) also refers to the danger of women handicapping themselves and states that

> in a 2004 survey, 40% of women said that it was much better for everyone involved if the man is the achiever outside the home and the woman takes care of the household. I trust most women lawyers have now evolved beyond such thinking.

This tendency to stereotype might have something to do with the fact that fewer women apply in fact for higher positions. According to Sánchez González (2012), only 40% of applications for positions of discretionary appointment are made by female judges. One of the reasons for this, according to the above-mentioned study "Mapping the representation ... ", is that women anticipate a failure to be appointed and therefore decide not to apply due to a lack of trust in their own abilities.

In fighting against these stereotypes, it might be worth remembering what Wollstonecraft (1792), considered an early feminist, stated:

> the answer is: let there be no coercion established in society—no laws that force people into this or that social role or situation. When that is achieved, the common law of gravity will hold sway and the sexes will fall into their proper places.

Difficulties for female judges in reconciling family and work life

The difficulties that female judges have to face in reconciling family and work life probably represents the most important reason as to why there is a glass ceiling at the highest levels of the Spanish judiciary.[6] It is understandable that some women tend to prefer the civil service (it gives them favourable working conditions, including maternal and parental leave, according to the study "Mapping the representation ... "); unfortunately, motherhood is also the reason why they are promoted less than their male colleagues, according to official statistics.

The Judicial Career Survey on the reconciliation of family life showed that in 2008, 46.3% judges (39.4% male, 51.4% female) believed that nothing had changed so far in relation to balancing personal and professional life. 36.8% judges (44.2% male, 31.3% female) believed that it was necessary to promote more measures, and 61.4% (52.7% male, 68% female) believed it was very necessary. Besides, 87.6% of the judges believed that the reconciliation of family and work life conditions a possible decision to promote. So it is clear, for the literature (Otero Parga, 2013; Gómez Bahillo *et al.*, 2016) and the judges themselves, that the women-mother role hinders their possibilities of competing with their male peers.

In relation to this some measures have been taken. Until 2011, *el Reglamento 1/1995 de la Carrera Judicial* established that the voluntary leave of absence to care for children which can last up to three years (differing from the legal leave), only guaranteed that applicants would keep their places, seniority and other status during the first year of leave. Nowadays, the new regulation (2011) extends this term to two years.

However, despite the Strategic Plan of 2013 including a series of measures in relation to reconciling family and work life, it seems that there have not been many changes. The VI National survey to all judges or magistrates in active service (2015) shows that 61% of judges (52% male, 74% female) believe that the General Board of the Judiciary does not facilitate the adoption and application of measures for reconciling family and work life. It also shows that 63% judges (53% male, 78% female) find it difficult to reconcile work with other personal and professional occupations.

The real problem is that, as the spokesperson of *Judges for Democracy*, Ignacio González, said, "women ask for more permits to take care of their house or their children and that is a reality".[7] The report on the structure of the judicial Career (January 2018) is very indicative: during 2017, 17 judges and magistrates were on voluntary leave for child care, of which 100% were women.

What is the solution then? Simone de Beauvoir (1975) wrote some years ago:

> no woman should be authorised to stay at home to raise her children. Society should be totally different. Women should not have that choice, precisely because if there is such a choice, too many women will make that one. It is a way of forcing women in a certain direction.

However, this might seem a radical solution. Professor Otero Parga (2013) considers that there should be the choice to stay at home but she also believes that it is fundamental to break stereotypes, to change patterns. This task corresponds to society as a whole and it will take time before it is completed. We need to do that little by little, without haste but without pause.

Conclusions

The existence of a glass ceiling at the highest levels of the Spanish judiciary and other European countries is undeniable. For that reason, the only possible conclusion is that the end of tokenism in the judiciary has not arrived yet. Cook (1978) said that "tokenism only promises its own perpetuation, i.e. that one woman only will be sitting in the same court in the next generation as in this generation", and apparently this is what is happening so far. We must make an effort to overcome this situation. The path and the advances that we have experienced in recent years are positive but much remains to be done.

Gloria Potayos, founder of the Spanish Female Judges Association, summarises the situation very well: there are no more female judges in the Supreme Court because the capacities and essential contributions of female judges are denied and the burden of care that women continue to suffer prevents them from competing with men.[8]

For this reason, we must reflect on the aforementioned causes focusing on sex discrimination and the difficulty in reconciling family and work life amongst others that may exist. We also need to reflect on the cultural misconceptions that surround women and the care of children or relatives and make a concerted effort to recognise and break stereotypes in order to overcome this glass ceiling.

In the aforementioned study "Mapping the representation ... " some positive solutions are offered. Among them, I will highlight three: introducing more flexible working conditions, continuing judicial education on gender equality and promoting networking and mentoring. It is important to enhance the capacity and infrastructure of the associations of female judges, because it can fulfil a solidarity and support function for individual women and can be a source of training and education. Also, in my opinion, it would be interesting to introduce gender quotas at the highest levels of the judiciary where the appointments are discretionary. Some authors argue that gender quotas would be counterproductive (Sánchez González 2012), but I disagree as there are plenty of highly qualified female judges. Ensuring that 40–60% of the members are female judges should not mean that they are chosen because they are women, but rather because they are highly competent women judges.

Notes

1. For more information: www.lavozdegalicia.es/noticia/galicia/2019/10/11/campana-contra-cgpj-falta-mujeres-terna-sala-civil-supremo/0003_201910G11P6991.htm; www.publico.es/politica/catedratica-descartada-supremo-favor-registrador-curriculum-inferior.html; and www.infolibre.es/noticias/opinion/plaza_publica/2019/10/05/que_meritos_no_han_tenerse_para_ser_magistrado_del_tribunal_supremo_99343_2003.html.
2. Inter alia, *The glass ceiling at the Supreme Court,* available at: www.cadenaser.com/ser/2018/03/02/tribunales/1520004269_287107; *The ignored presence of women in the judiciary,* available at: www.cadenaser.com/ser/2018/03/02/tribunales/1519994779_776674.html; *Women only represent the 14 percent in the Supreme Court,* available at: www.nuevatribuna.es/articulo/espana/mujeres-solo-ocupan-14-puestos-tribunal-supremo/20180119075531147467.html.
3. *The Madrid* newspaper said on the 27th march 1971 that Carmen Venero becoming a family judge corresponded to "the characteristics, qualities and aptitudes with which femininity has been millennially adorned".
4. For more information: www.publico.es/sociedad/mujeres-representan-70-8-jueces-ultima-promocion.html
5. On the one hand, Coontz (2000) wrote that "when asked whether women judges decide cases differently by virtue of being female, Minnesota Supreme Court Justice Jeanne Coyne replied that, in her experience, a wise old man and a wise old woman reach the same conclusion". On the other hand, Wald (2013) believed that this is not true, and in her opinion, considering that women and men make the same legal decision is actually a myth. Besides, this theory of a different voice should be nuanced. Wilson (1990) said that "there are probably whole areas of the law on which there is no uniquely feminine perspective. This is not to say that the development of the law in these areas has not been influenced by the fact that lawyers and judges have all been men. Rather, the principles and the underlying premises are so firmly entrenched and so fundamentally sound that no good would be achieved by attempting to re-invent the wheel, even if the revised version did have a few more spokes in it. I have in mind areas such as the law of contract, the law of real property, and the law applicable to corporations". In my opinion, this is not entirely true, because as García Rubio (2014) has shown, some legal categories, including contract and commercial law, do not properly reflect women's experiences.

6. The difficulty in reconciling family and work life is present in another Judiciaries. Williams and Thames (2008) argued that "we expect that the greater the percentage of women participating in the labor force, and the lower the fertility rate, the higher the political participation of women. (...). Fewer children will also make it easier for women to participate in public life". Also, Cook (1978) stated that "child-bearing is the traditional female role and earning salaries outside the domestic institution is non-traditional. It is logical that women judges would be more acceptable when and where the populace views the role of women less traditionally. There is a strong relationship between these variables; the higher women's incomes in the state, the more women judges; the lower the birth rate, the more women judges". Connelly and Hilliard (1993) stated that "the careers of women in the legal profession, as in other areas of employment, are frequently dominated by the responsibilities of parenthood. As a result, many women lawyers experience a broken career path, and part-time and locum work is much more common among women than among men".
7. cadenaser.com/ser/2018/03/02/tribunales/1519994779_776674.html
8. cadenaser.com/ser/2018/03/02/tribunales/1519994779_776674.html

Disclosure statement

No potential conflict of interest was reported by the author(s).

Funding

This work was supported by Consellería de Cultura, Educación e Ordenación Universitaria, Xunta de Galicia, 10.13039/501100008425, grant no. ED481B-2019-039.

ORCID

Mónica García Goldar http://orcid.org/0000-0002-3235-292X

References

Ammerman Yebra, J. (2017) *Las madres solas ante los tribunales, la administración y las leyes: ¿se perpetúa la discriminación?* (Valencia, Tirant to Blanch).

Arbour, L. (1993) Femmes de jugement et d'opinion, in: H. Dumont (Ed) *Femmes et Droite: 50 ans de vie commune et tout un avenir* (Montreal, Éditions Thémis), pp. 37–46.

Beauvoir, S. & Friedan, B. (1975) A dialogue, *The Saturday review. Sex, Society and the Female Dilemma, June 14*, pp. 12–21.

Collado Mateo, C. (2006) Mujeres, poder y derecho, *Feminismo/s, 8*, pp. 15–34.

Connelly, A. & Hilliard, B. (1993) *Gender and the Law in Ireland* (Dublin, Oak Tree Press).

Cook, B.C. (1978) Women judges: the end of Tokenism, in: W. Hepperle & L. Crites (Eds) *Women in the Courts* (Williamsburg, Va. National Center for State Courts), pp. 84–105.

Coontz, P. (2000) Gender and judicial decisions: do female judges decide cases differently than male judges?, *Gender Issues, 18*, pp. 59–73.

Fix, M. P. & Johnson, G. E. (2017) Public perceptions of gender bias in the decisions of female state court judges, *Vanderbilt Law Review, 70*, pp. 1845–1886.

Forell, C. & Matthews, D. M. (2000) *A law of her own: The Reasonable Woman as a Measure of man* (New York, New York University Press).

García Rubio, M.P. (2014) Comprender y transmitir el derecho de las mujeres, in: C. Mesa Marrero & M.C. Grau Pineda (Eds), *Mujeres, contratos y empresa desde la igualdad de género* (Valencia, Tirant lo Blanch), pp. 77–92.

Gómez Bahillo, C., Elboj Saso, C. & Marcén Muñío, C. (2016) The feminization of the Spanish judiciary, *Convergencia: revista de ciencias sociales, 70*, pp. 199–226.

Kenney, S. J. (2013) *Gender and Justice: Why Women in the Judiciary Really Matter* (New York, Routledge).

Lorente Acosta, M. (2014) *Tú haz la comida, que yo cuelgo los cuadros. Trampas y tramposos en la cultura de la desigualdad* (Barcelona, Planeta).

Maule, L. S. (2000) A different voice. The feminine jurisprudence of the Minnesota State Supreme Court, *Buffalo Women's Law Journal*, 9, pp. 295–316.

Otero Parga, M. (2013) Una mujer juez. A propósito del Plan 14/02/2013 de Igualdad de la Carrera Judicial, *Dereito: revista xurídica da Universidade de Santiago de Compostela, 22*, pp. 441–474.

Rhode, D. (1987) Justice, gender and the Justices, in: L. Crites (Ed) *Women, the Courts and Equality* (Beverly Hills, Sage), pp. 13–34.

Sánchez González, A. (2012) Pasado y presente de la mujer en la judicatura, in: A. Gallardo Rodríguez (coord.), A. Figuerelo Burrieza, M. Del Pozo Pérez & M. León Alonso (dirs.), *Igualdad: retos para el siglo XXI*, (Santiago de Compostela, Andavira), pp. 309–318.

Schultz, U., *et al.* (2013) *Gender and Judging* (Oxford, Hart).

Valpuesta Fernández, R. (2016) *La construcción de un pensamiento crítico* (Sevilla, Aconcagua).

Wald, P. M. (2013) Myths about womeńs career in law, *The University of Baltimore Journal of International Law, 2*(2013–2014), pp. 1–17.

Williams, M. S. & Thames, F. C. (2008) Women's representation on high courts in advanced industrialized countries, *Politics and Gender, 4*, pp. 451–471.

Wilson, B. (1990) Will women judges really make a difference?, *Osgoode Hall Law Journal, 28* (3), pp. 507–522.

Wollstonecraft, M. (1792) *A Vindication of the Rights of the Woman.* Available at: pinkmonkey.com/dl/library1/vindicat.pdf, accessed 15 March 2018.

Electronic resources

Catalyst study. (2007) The double-bind dilemma for women in leadership: damned if you do, doomed if you don't. Available at: https://www.catalyst.org/wp-content/uploads/2019/01/The_Double_Bind_Dilemma_for_Women_in_Leadership_Damned_if_You_Do_Doomed_if_You_Dont.pdf.

Consejo General del Poder Judicial. (2008) Encuesta a la Carrera judicial sobre la conciliación de la vida familiar. Available at: http://www.poderjudicial.es/stfls/ESTADISTICA%20JUDICIAL%20NUEVO/FICHEROS/9001%20Encuestas%20a%20la%20Carrera%20Judicial/A%C3%B1os%20anteriores/Encuesta%20carrera%20judicial%202008%20conciliacion%20vida%20familiar.pdf.

Consejo General del Poder Judicial. (2013) Plan de Igualdad de la Carrera Judicial. Available at: http://www.poderjudicial.es/stfls/CGPJ/COMISI%C3%93N%20DE%20IGUALDAD/20130409%20Plan%20de%20igualdad%20de%20la%20Carrera%20Judicial.pdf.

Consejo General del Poder Judicial. (2015) VI Encuesta de ámbito nacional a todos los jueces o magistrados en servicio activo. Available at: http://www.poderjudicial.es/stfls/SALA%20DE%20PRENSA/NOTAS%20DE%20PRENSA/20150925%20INFORME%20CGPJ.pdf.

Consejo General del Poder Judicial. (2018) Informe sobre la estructura de la Carrera judicial a 1 de enero de 2018. Available at: http://www.poderjudicial.es/stfls/ESTADISTICA/FICHEROS/2002%20Caracteristicas%20de%20jueces%20y%20magistrados/A%C3%B1os%20anteriores/Carrera%20Judicial%202018.pdf.

Consejo General del Poder Judicial. (2020) II Plan de Igualdad de la Carrera Judicial. Available at: http://www.poderjudicial.es/stfls/CGPJ/COMISI%C3%93N%20DE%20IGUALDAD/20200131%20Plan%20de%20igualdad%20de%20la%20Carrera%20Judicial.pdf.

European Comission. (1998) One hundred words for equality. Available at: https://publications.europa.eu/en/publication-detail/-/publication/7342d801-86cc-4f59-a71a-2ff7c0e04123/language-en.

Novo Canto, S. I. (2014) The glass ceiling in the Spanish judiciary. Available at: https://timeforequality.org/dossier-women-and-the-judiciary-in-italy/donne-e-magistratura-in-italia-e-nel-mondo-en/the-glass-ceiling-in-the-spanish-judiciary/.

Problems in the pathways to judicial success: women in the legal profession in Northern Ireland

Leah Treanor

ABSTRACT
This paper considers women's representation in the under-explored context of the judiciary in Northern Ireland. Previous research into the experiences of women practitioners in the legal profession in Northern Ireland has indicated that women are discouraged from pursuing judicial careers for a variety of reasons associated with their gender. Further research into the gendered barriers these women practitioners face is required in order to assess the extent to which the same may impede their career progression. This paper uses a critical, social constructionist feminist approach to explore some of the gendered barriers influencing women's under-representation in Northern Ireland's judiciary. It is contended that representation can only be improved when women's retention and progression through the ranks of the legal profession is addressed. Employing gender as a lens, this paper will analyse potential difficulties faced by the women solicitors and barristers in Northern Ireland in order to assess future judicial gender parity prospects in this jurisdiction as it is these women solicitors and barristers who form the female "talent pool" from which future members of the judiciary will be selected.

Introduction

The absence of women in the legal profession is, arguably, most readily visible at judicial level. Patterns of male-dominance in the judiciary are replicated across several jurisdictions (CEPEJ, 2016). Thus, it is perhaps unsurprising that the relationship between gender and the judiciary is one which attracts much academic interest in jurisdictions across the globe (Rackley, 2013; Valdini and Shortell, 2016; Bessière and Mille, 2014; McLoughlin, 2015; Crandall, 2014).

Whilst there have been some notable works considering gender and the Northern Irish judiciary (Feenan, 2005; Leith *et al.*, 2013; Morison, 2015), there is a comparative scarcity of research centring on the women solicitors and barristers who form the "talent pool" from which future judges are drawn. This conceptual paper adopts the working hypothesis that it is only through addressing the difficulties women face in the pathways to judicial careers, that real progress, in terms of diversity in the demography of the Northern Ireland judiciary, can be realised. This paper calls for future research using gender as a "lens" (Ahl, 2004; Marlow *et al.*, 2009) to explore some of the potential explanations for women's disproportionate attrition from legal practice and the gendered obstacles they may face in continuing professional practice in Northern Ireland.

This paper will begin by outlining the professional legal landscape in Northern Ireland. It will then move on to consider the demographic of the Northern Ireland judiciary and the initiatives which have sought to enhance judicial diversity in this jurisdiction. This will set the context for the subsequent discussion of the realities of practice for the women barristers and solicitors who represent the women judges of the future.

Northern Ireland in context

Following the partition of Ireland, two separate legal jurisdictions were created on the island: Ireland and Northern Ireland. Comparatively speaking, Northern Ireland is a very small jurisdiction, serving a population of approximately 1.8 million (NISRA, 2017). However, notwithstanding its size, there are 782 barristers and over 2,300 solicitors qualified to practice law in Northern Ireland, (Bar Library, 2019; Law Society of Northern Ireland, 2019).

In many jurisdictions, there is just one kind of professional legal practitioner e.g. *l'avocat* in France or *the lawyer* in the United States. In Northern Ireland, however, there are two separate branches of the legal profession: solicitors and barristers. Arguably, the distinction between the two is becoming increasingly academic. However, for present purposes, the key distinction lies in the structural differences between the professions. Unlike solicitors, barristers are self-employed. They are not permitted to form partnerships, to incorporate, nor to advertise. References herein to the "legal profession" encompass both solicitors and barristers. Where it is necessary to draw distinctions between the two, the appropriate titles will be construed accordingly.

At present, none of Northern Ireland's most senior judges (i.e. none of the 4 judges in the Northern Ireland Court of Appeal) are women. In 2015, the first two women were appointed to the High Court Bench (Judiciary NI, 2019). This was the first time since 1921, when the two jurisdictions were first established in Ireland, that Northern Ireland has had a woman High Court Judge; the other 7 High Court Justices are men. Whilst it has taken almost a century for women to penetrate the upper echelons of the Northern Irish judiciary, the picture becomes slightly more promising as one descends the tiers of the judiciary. At County Court level, 6 of the 18 sitting County Court Judges in Northern Ireland are women. At District Judge level, just 9 of all 25 sitting District Judges are women, (Judiciary NI, 2019). Thus, overall, women account for 30% of current judicial office holders in Northern Ireland, (Judiciary NI, 2019). But what, if anything, is being done to address the visible lack of women in our judiciary?

Northern Ireland Judicial Appointments Commission

In order to combat the under-representation of women in the judiciary, many jurisdictions have established specific bodies tasked with handling judicial appointments.[1] Northern Ireland's Judicial Appointments Commission ("NIJAC") was established in 2005 with the aim of ensuring transparency in judicial appointments and providing a diverse judiciary, reflective of the society it serves. In Northern Ireland, it is a statutory requirement that "the selection of a person to be appointed, or recommended for appointment, to a listed judicial office ... must be made solely on the basis of merit".[2] The explicit reliance on merit as the *sole* criterion for judicial appointments is, arguably, problematic due to its inherent scope for unconscious bias (Davis and Williams, 2003; Malleson, 2006; Thornton, 2007). Owing to the innate equivocality of merit, it has been suggested that it is susceptible to both "misidentification and misinterpretation" (Rackley, 2013, p. 193); often, along gendered lines. As such, merit may, consciously or otherwise, be used as a "mask through which stereotypes and heuristic biases operate" (Iyer, 2013).

Somewhat unhelpfully, the legislation conferring power of appointment on NIJAC does not substantively engage with the concept of merit; failing to offer either definition or criteria for its assessment. In any event, as the experience in England and Wales would appear to suggest, the provision of criteria, of itself, does not preclude criticism on the basis of ambiguity. Indeed, it has been argued that such "criteria might be fleshed out in a way that means men are more likely to display a characteristic than women" (Rackley, 2013) as "even seemingly neutral merit criteria can be subverted by masculine bias" (Iyer, p. 116). If such criticisms can be made of systems in which efforts *have* been made to delineate the scope of merit, it is not difficult to envisage the implications for Northern Ireland.

Research considering the effectiveness of judicial appointments committees concluded that whilst, at the outset, such committees may have positive outcomes for women, their effectiveness wanes over time (Iyer, p. 114). It has been suggested that this may be due to merit commissions unconsciously "over-compensating" for previous male bias in the earlier years, though this is unproven (Iyer, 2013). In the context of Northern Ireland, a recent report indicated that Northern Ireland had one of the lowest proportions of women in judicial power in Europe (Cromie, 2014). Perhaps somewhat embarrassingly, this report post-dates the establishment of NIJAC by almost 10 years.

Whilst research considering whether women perform better when merit commissions are used has been somewhat inconclusive (Iyer, p. 105), critical feminist evaluation of the concept of merit, as operationalised by such bodies, arguably goes some distance in explaining why this may not be the case. Acknowledging merit as a product of social construction, Malleson (2006, p. 391) contends that

that which constitutes evidence of merit "can only ever be determined with reference to the nature of the recruitment pool as a whole". She argues that,

> as the definition of what constitutes evidence of merit adapts to reflect changes in the experiences and career patterns of the recruitment pool ... the potential pool itself adapts as groups and individuals opt in and out, making early and mid-career choices on the basis of whether they see themselves as likely to be well-qualified and favoured candidates. (Malleson (2006)

The process of constructing merit is thus both transactional and "dynamic" (Thornton, 2007). This maintains sufficient space for merit's problematic subjectivity to thrive; thereby permitting the misidentification and misinterpretation referred to earlier and, in turn, undermining "the argument that diversity and equality can be achieved by application of a neutral or unbiased notion of merit" (Malleson, 2006, p. 392).

Merit, gender and judicial appointments

A recent study into the role of merit in judicial appointment in Northern Ireland found that, generally speaking, many were sceptical as to whether NIJAC was, in fact, rewarding "merit". Respondents indicated that, in the context of Northern Ireland, demonstration of merit requires both "a certain background and particular expertise" (Leith *et al.*, 2013, p. 5). In particular, merit was "widely seen as based on qualities mainly possessed by the bar ... based on seniority and experience of advocacy in court" (Leith *et al.*, 2013). Furthermore, "women generally believed themselves to be less likely to be seen as having this sort of merit or ... the opportunities to gain it" (Leith *et al.*, 2013). Interestingly, it also concluded that, in Northern Ireland, "generally female merit is something different and does not seem to be transferable" (Leith *et al.*, 2013, p. 53).

Whilst this notion of "female merit" remains undefined, such findings appear to support the notion that merit *is* gendered. It is suggested that, in seeking to identify and fully understand this relationship, it is necessary to explore the experiences of the women legal practitioners who represent the prospective judicial talent pool. It is argued herein that, in doing so, it is appropriate to utilise gender as a lens to permit exploration of both the gendered nature of women's individual experiences and of the professions within which they operate.

For social constructionists, gender is understood in the context of the cultural roles and expectations associated with the sexes, as opposed to a biological identity. As such, gender is not a static characteristic which can be possessed by an individual. Rather, it is a dynamic, performative process by which such cultural expectations are both produced and re-produced through behaviour (Butler, 1990).

Understanding gender in this way permits greater depth of analysis in terms of the construction of both individual gendered identities and of the gendering of organisations and professions. This is possible through moving away from the traditional gender dichotomy towards a more flexible and nuanced view of how gender operates. The conflation of sex and gender creates a temptation to utilise gender as a mere variable in order to facilitate comparison between the sexes. However, in the area of gender and the professions, there have been several recent calls for a more sophisticated approach to undertaking feminist research utilising gender as a "lens" (Ahl 2004; Marlow *et al.*, 2009). Employing gender as a lens in feminist research permits the researcher to explore women's experiences and seeks to counter the normative androcentric approach to sociological research of the past, wherein women were either "invisible" or were presented as the "underside" of male lives, culture and experiences (McCarl Nielsen, 1990 p. 10; DuBois, 1983 p. 110). In order to ensure that women are appropriately represented, research exploring *their* experiences is necessary. In the absence of such research emanating from Northern Ireland, research considering the experiences of women lawyers in other jurisdictions is instructive. At this juncture, some of the key themes discernible therefrom will be explored and contrasted with the extant literature relating to Northern Ireland.

Eligibility

The apparent homogeneity of the judicial talent pool in Northern Ireland may, partially, be attributed to the fact that many women may be at a disadvantage in terms of attaining the requisite length and breadth of experience necessary to take judicial office. In order to become eligible to become a Judge in Northern Ireland, one must have been in practice as a lawyer for a period of *at least* seven years. This requirement, of itself, may serve to limit the number of eligible women, particularly in the context of those located within the self-employed Bar which presents its own difficulties in terms of women's ability to sustain careers for such extended periods. It is unfortunate that there is a lack of contemporary research considering gendered patterns of attrition from the profession in Northern Ireland. However, membership figures themselves are somewhat telling. Of the 782 barristers holding current practising certificates for the year 2018/2019, just 269 are women (34.4%) (The Bar Library, 2019).

Generally speaking, judges are more likely to be male and are less likely to have practised as solicitors before coming to the bench (Rackley, 2013, p. 79). The view that the Bar is the "traditional route into the judiciary in the eyes of much of the legal profession" (Constitution Committee, 2017) is not novel. Acknowledging this, Lord Neuberger (2017) recently said, "there is still an inbuilt assumption that it will tend to be a barrister, not a solicitor, who becomes a High Court judge … ". Indeed, it is clear that this view prevails in Northern Ireland, wherein appointments to the High Court are seen as "the final phase of a career at the Bar" (Leith *et al.*, 2013). Interestingly, when asked about that which constitutes "merit" in the context of judicial appointments, many solicitor respondents felt that too much weight was placed on advocacy as a requirement (Leith *et al.*, 2013). Thus, it is clear, that the manner in which judicial "merit" is constructed in Northern Ireland is problematic and may preserve the homogeneity of the judicial talent pool through encouraging suitably qualified solicitors to self-select out of the recruitment process or, alternatively, through disadvantaging those in certain practice areas.

Gendered occupational segregation

In addition to potential difficulties in attaining the length of experience necessary, undoubtedly of even greater significance is the difficulty in attaining the quality and/or type of experience necessary to demonstrate "judicial merit". A recurring theme in the literature on gender and the legal profession is the segregation of women into certain types of legal work, in particular, family law (Leith *et al.*, 2013, p. 53). Such sex-typing of work continues to affect even those women who are successful in their appointments to judicial roles, with many women reporting that they experienced explicit discrimination in the form of gendered work allocation (Canadian Bar Association, 1993). Anecdotally, this would appear to be the experience of women in private practice at the Bar of Northern Ireland, wherein women are disproportionately represented in family law practice. The literature on the sex-typing of work is instructive insofar as such practices may be related to wider, macro-level conceptualisations of the "female".

The familiar notion of women having a natural propensity for caring and nurturing is closely related to the sex-typing of certain work (Bradley, 2010). Women's disproportionate over-representation in family law may be attributed to essentialist assumptions about women's suitability for such work which, typically, concerns children, families and vulnerable individuals. In addition, from a practical perspective, such work also involves a greater deal of "pastoral" client care work. The assumption that women are more naturally suited to practice areas involving such emotional labour, which may be viewed as an extension of their domestic caring roles, is undoubtedly derived from macro-level gender schema (Bradley, 2010). This has the result of preserving and justifying gendered divisions of labour within the profession (Acker, 1990; Witz, 1991).

However, such occupational segregation may serve to impede women's careers on a more fundamental level. Unlike criminal or commercial practice, employment and family practice offer fewer advocacy opportunities and carry less prestige. It is fair to suggest that women's segregation into such practice areas may prevent them from attaining the required degree of advocacy experience (Davis and Williams, 2003) or, indeed, the required degree of "visible" and "accepted" advocacy experience necessary to evidence merit. This is particularly true in the case of family law practice wherein the knowledge, skills and experience of practitioners are often trivialised and undermined. Indeed, the potential for family matters to settle out of Court may also serve to reduce the advocacy opportunities available to practitioners therein (Douglas, 2018).

It may be that a failure to value work such as family law, typically undertaken by women practitioners, renders it less valuable in terms of demonstrating the sort of qualities, skills and experience which have come to constitute merit in judicial appointments in Northern Ireland. This, coupled with the apparent ease with which merit can be recognised in men who fit the "traditional criteria", can only serve to perpetuate masculine homogeneity within the profession. Through reproducing widely-held essentialist ascriptions, such practices serve to reinforce the notion of women as natural "carers" more suited to emotional work, thereby subjugating the feminine and, by corollary, reinforcing the prevailing narrative of the ideal professional as "male" (Bolton and Muzio, 2008; Acker 1990). This gendered division of labour permits the subordination of women practitioners in the legal profession (Sommerlad and Sanderson, 1998; Hagan and Kay, 1995). Thus, work such as family law is not only de-valued in comparison to traditionally male-dominated practice areas but, also, contributes to the "othering" of women within the profession (Bolton and Muzio, 2008).

The "motherhood penalty"

A second theme from the literature concerns the relationship between work and domestic/caring responsibilities, which can be problematic for those aspiring to a judicial career. Despite both part-time and deputised judicial roles offering greater flexibility, life on the bench is often regarded as incompatible with domestic obligations. A recent study found that a "lack of flexibility in working practices on the Bench" was the most commonly cited barrier to judicial appointment (Turenne and Bell, 2018). Perhaps unsurprisingly, the majority of women respondents raised this as an issue (65% as compared with 24% of men).[3] The perceived inflexibility in judicial working patterns is identified with regard to working hours and, further, geographical deployment and specialism.[4]

The notion that "a part-time approach to judicial appointments" does not align with what is "required for a judicial post (i.e. a full commitment to the role)" appears to endure.[5] In a previous study in Northern Ireland, respondents indicated that

> … fulfilling family duties; seeking a few disparate judicial roles; not being focused on a judicial career were all viewed as undermining the respondents view of whether a candidate had merit or not. The judge, in this light, is never part of society – always apart and always focused on the needs of the judicial task.[6]

It is clear from the literature that inflexibility in working patterns, in all its forms, is particularly important to women. It has been suggested that perceptions of inflexibility in this regard can and does discourage suitably qualified women from pursuing judicial roles (Feenan, 2005; Mack and Anleu 2014). In 2010, the Advisory Panel on Judicial Diversity recommended that "it should be assumed that all posts are capable of being delivered through some form of flexible working arrangements, with exceptions needing justifying". Notwithstanding this recommendation, at present "part-time working is not clearly addressed by any of the Judicial Appointments Commissions in their advertisements, though the Northern Irish Commission at least opens up that possibility" (Turenne and Bell, 2018).

Generally speaking, the majority of requests for part-time work or flexible working arrangements are made by women and arise from maternity leave and domestic and/or care-giving responsibilities (Law Institute of Victoria, 2006). The effect of a move to part-time or flexible working can often be seen in the quality of work offered to those availing of such arrangements. In the context of legal practice, it would appear that those transitioning to part-time/flexible work can expect stalled career progression (Law Institute of Victoria, 2006, p. 159), less autonomy and responsibility and, in some cases, being allocated work in a different field of law (AEQUUS Partners, 2005). Such outcomes reflect the enduring "stigma" associated with part-time workers generally, namely, that they are less committed (Fuchs-Epstein *et al.*, 1999). This perceived failure to prioritise work, and thereby to conform to gendered norms of the "ideal worker", serves to undermine part-time solicitors' contributions to the workplace, rendering them invisible. This, in turn, positions them as lacking the commitment required to progress to partnership (Williams and Calvert, 2002). It has been reported that requests to work part-time are not always well-received and can have consequences with regard to the career advancement of women solicitors aspiring to partnership (Campbell and Chalmers 2011, p. 157). The advent of so-called "mommy track" (Jacobs, 2014), whereby women are effectively "opted-out" of the running for partnership and retained at associate level following childbirth, represents a worrying development in the landscape of legal practice.

Indeed, women barristers availing of maternity leave have reported similar detriments to their practices upon return. In the context of the self-employed Bar, maternity leave has been described as "career suicide", with women barristers facing returning "to nothing except a devastated practice" (The Guardian, 2011). Recognition of the particular difficulties faced by self-employed women barristers availing of maternity leave prompted the Bar Standards Board of England and Wales to issue revised equality and diversity guidance pertaining to parental leave policies in what has been described as a "watershed moment" (Simmons, 2017).

"The motherhood penalty" (Sterling, 2016) whilst not specific to the practice of law, is a recurring theme in the literature relating to legal practice (Pinnington and Sandberg, 2013; Reichman and Sterling, 2002; Walsh, 2013) and serves as a closure mechanism, blocking off women's routes to career progression. Interestingly, it would appear that the motherhood penalty extends even to those who are not mothers (Budig and Hodges, 2014; Gough and Noonan, 2013). Cockburn (1991) describes how women, generally, are "defined in domesticity… even if the woman… is celibate or childless she is seen and represented as one of the maternal sex" (Cockburn, 1991, p. 76). Research in other professional contexts suggests a wider tendency to assume that women's priorities lie in the domestic realm, as opposed to within their professional careers; as a result, women, as professionals, are perceived as less "committed" than men (Fuchs Epstein *et al.*, 2013; Twenge, 2010). A full exploration of the relationship between such gendered notions of commitment is out-with the ambit of this paper. However, it may be argued that a changing legal marketplace has conferred an enhanced significance on "commitment" as currency, particularly in relation to demonstrating "merit".

In considering the legal services sector, Wald (2010) refers to that which he calls a "hypercompetitive" work ethic whereby individuals are expected to demonstrate commitment through maximum availability to deal with clients. In practical terms, this often means ensuring availability to deal with phone calls and emails in the evenings or at weekends – a prospect much less challenging for the unencumbered "ideal" (male) worker (Acker, 1990). These structural changes intersect with cultural changes in the legal marketplace which have been described as a move towards "commercialized professionalization" (Hanlon, 1999). This notion of commercialised professionalism embodies the more "entrepreneurial" approach to legal service provision which has appeared to dominate in recent times. This, alongside the redefinition of merit as temporal commitment, may present particular difficulties for women solicitors as time, in a professional context, is often a gendered resource.

Reluctance to apply for judicial roles

Reflecting a wider "recruitment crisis" within the UK judiciary, the Lord Chief Justice for Northern Ireland has recently acknowledged recruitment difficulties in Northern Ireland (SSRB, 2017). Whilst these have been attributed to various factors, e.g. judicial pension changes, loss of respect for the judiciary, remuneration and workload (Morison and Dickson, 2019; Turenne and Bell, 2018), it would appear that there is a specific problem recruiting women.

We have seen how the homogeneity of the judicial talent pool may be, in part, explained by the masculine notions of merit underpinning recruitment and, by corollary, the homosocial reproduction this permits. However, the reasons for women's apparent reluctance to apply for judicial roles warrants further exploration. Research has indicated that women require more encouragement than men to apply for such roles (Feenan, 2005, p. 6). Universally, the so-called confidence gap means that, unlike their male colleagues, many women often do not apply for roles unless they fulfil 100 per cent of the criteria (Clark, 2014; Mohr, 2014).

Relatedly, it may also be the case that many women are deterred from pursuing judicial appointment due to their perceptions of the bench as male-dominated (Genn, 2017). Generally speaking, the internalisation of macro-level gendered schema plays an important role in shaping individual perceptions of available opportunities (Wilson, 2003; Baughn *et al.*, 2006; Welter and Smallbone, 2008.) This can encourage individuals to make gender-congruent choices which, in turn, can serve to re-produce those gendered norms (Evans and Diekman, 2009). For instance, the male-dominated nature of the judiciary may contribute to the notion that judicial business is "men's work" and may discourage women from pursuing judicial careers due to perceptions of limited possibilities for women therein (Blanton, 2001). The judiciary is, undoubtedly, sex-typed as a "male" profession with "the judge" conjuring images of "man". Such traditional masculine bias inevitably results in women being perceived as "non-judicial" (Rackley, 2013, p. 602) with the double bind that women who do satisfy masculine merit are seen as "too aggressive" (Davis and Williams, 2003, p. 832). This positioning of women as "non-judicial" or "other" may go some distance in explaining why male candidates appear to be preferred; it may be that it is easier to recognise merit in those who resemble current judicial office-holders, of which the majority are men. In addition, perceptions about "the ethos of the back corridor" (Leith *et al.*, 2013; Morison, 2015) and reports of women judges experiencing exclusion at the hands of their male-majority colleagues (Solberg, 2006) represent tangible deterrents for would-be women judges.

Conclusion

This paper offers an overview of the extant literature relating to gender and the legal profession. It is clear that there are number of factors which conspire to sustain women's under-representation in the judiciary in Northern Ireland and that efforts made, thus far, to re-dress the balance have been less than effective. Even so, it must be borne in mind that any solution to women's under-representation at judicial level must address those issues which impede women's career progression across all branches of the legal profession. General assumptions about men and women appear to be influential in shaping both notions of what it means to be a legal professional and, also, the types of work which are appropriate for men and women. It is clear that further research is required into the gendered division of labour within professional legal practice and the potential implications thereof for the career progression of these women professionals. It is hoped that future research considering these women's experiences in legal professional practice will further our understanding the reasons for women's poor representation at judicial level and, importantly, the most effective means by which this issue can be addressed.

Whilst there appears to have been something of a recognition of the need for greater diversity within the Northern Irish judiciary in recent times, there remains a distance yet to travel. It is hoped that exploration of the experiences of women in professional legal practice in Northern Ireland will provide a roadmap for future travel, as "a diverse judiciary is an indispensable requirement of any democracy" (International Association of Women Judges, 2006).

Notes

1. For instance, Scotland's Judicial Appointments Board was established in 2002, England's in 2006 and similar measures were adopted in Australia in 2008.
2. Justice (Northern Ireland) Act 2002 s5(8).
3. Turenne and Bell (2018).
4. Turenne and Bell (n 20).
5. Queen's University (n 10) 6.
6. Queen's University (n 10) 48.

Disclosure statement

No potential conflict of interest was reported by the author(s).

References

Acker, J. (1990) Hierarchies, jobs, bodies: a theory of gendered organisations, *Gender and Society,* 4(2), pp. 139–158.

Advisory Panel on Judicial Diversity (2010) Report (Chair Dame J. Neuberger).

AEQUUS Partners (2005) *A 360° Review: Flexible Work Practices: Confronting Myths and Realities in the Legal Profession* (Melbourne, Victorian Women Lawyers).

Ahl, H. (2004) *The Scientific Reproduction of Gender Inequality: A Discourse Analysis of Research Texts on Women's Entrepreneurship* (Hendon, Copenhagen Business School Press).

Bar Library (2019) Practising barristers. Available at: http://www.barofni.com/page/practising-barristers, accessed 18 January 2019.

Baughn, C., Chua, B. & Neupert, K. (2006) The normative context for women's participation in entrepreneurship: a multicountry study, *Entrepreneurship Theory & Practice*, 30(5), pp. 687–708.

Bessière, C. & Mille, M. (2014) Le Juge est (Souvent) une Femme, *Sociologie du Travail*, 55, pp. 341–368.

Blanton, H. (2001) Evaluating the self in the context of another: the three selves model of social comparison, assimilation and contrast, in: G. Moskowitz (Ed) *Cognitive Social Psychology: The Princeton Symposium on the Legacy and Future of Social Cognition* (Mahwah, Erlbaum), pp. 75–87.

Bolton, S. & Muzio, D. (2008) The paradoxical processes of feminization in the professions: the case of established, aspiring and semi-professions, *Work, Employment and Society*, 22 (2), pp. 281–299.

Bradley, H. (2010) *Gender: Key Concepts* (Cambridge, Polity Press).

Budig, M. & Hodges, M. (2014) Statistical models and empirical evidence for differences in the motherhood penalty across the earnings distribution, *American Sociological Review*, 79 (2), pp. 358–364.

Butler, J. (1990) *Gender Trouble: Feminism and the Subversion of Identity* (New York, Routledge).

Campbell, I. & Chalmers, J. (2011) Part-time of what? Job quality and part-time employment in the legal profession in Australia, *Journal of Sociology*, 19(3), pp. 487–500.

Canadian Bar Association (1993) *Touchstones for Change: Equality, Diversity and Accountability* (Ottawa, Canadian Bar Association).

CEPEJ. (2016) *European Judicial Systems: Efficiency and Quality of Justice*. Available at: https://www.coe.int/t/dghl/cooperation/cepej/evaluation/2016/publication/CEPEJ%20Study%2023%20report%20EN%20web.pdf, accessed 22 May 2018.

Clark, N. (2014) Act now to shrink the confidence gap, *Forbes*, 28 April. Available at: http://www.forbes.com/sites/womensmedia/2014/04/28/act-now-to-shrink-the-confidence-gap/#3a81a2e14509, accessed 18 September 2016.

Cockburn, C. (1991) *In the Way of Women: Men's Resistance to Sex Equality in Organisations* (London, Macmillan).

Constitution Committee (2017) Judicial appointments: follow-up (HL 2017-19, 7).

Crandall, E. (2014) Does the system of judicial appointment matter? Exploring women's representation on Ontario's courts, *Canadian Journal of Women and the Law*, 26(2), pp. 185–205.

Cromie, C. (2014) Northern Ireland among lowest for female judges, *Belfast Telegraph*. Available at: https://www.belfasttelegraph.co.uk/woman/news/northern-ireland-among-lowest-for-female-judges-30651405.html, accessed 16 January 2018.

Davis, R. & Williams, G. (2003) Reform of the judicial appointments process: gender and the bench of the High Court of Australia, *Melbourne University Law Review*, 27, pp. 819–863.

Douglas, G. (2018) *Obligation and Commitment in Family Law* (Oxford, Hart Publishing).

DuBois, B. (1983) Passionate scholarship: notes on values, knowing and method in social science, in: G. Bowles & R. Duelli Klein (Eds) *Theories of Women's Studies* (London, Routledge & Kegan Paul), pp. 105–116.

Evans, C. & Diekman, A. (2009) On motivated role selection: gender beliefs, distant goals and career interest, *Psychology of Women Quarterly*, 33(2), pp. 235–249.

Feenan, D. (2005) *Applications by Women for Silk and Judicial Office in Northern Ireland*. Available at: http://cjani.courtsni.gov.uk/CJANIResearchReport.pdf, accessed 24 January 2016.

Fuchs-Epstein, C., Seron, C., Oglensky, B & Sauté, R. (1999) *The Part Time Paradox: Time Norms, Professional Lives, Family and Gender* (New York, Routledge).

Fuchs Epstein, C., Seron, C., Oglensky, B & Sauté, R. (2013) *The Part-Time Paradox: Time Norms, Professional Life, Family and Gender* (Oxford, Routledge).

Genn, H. (2017) The attractiveness of senior judicial appointment to highly qualified practitioners: report to the Judicial Executive Board, *Directorate of Judicial Offices for England and Wales*. Available at: https://www.ucl.ac.uk/laws/judicial-institute/files/The_Attractiveness_of_Senior_Judicial_Appointment_Research_Report.pdf 10/02/17, accessed 15 February 2017.

Gough, M. & Noonan, M (2013) A review of the motherhood wage penalty in the United States, *Sociology Compass*, 7(4), pp. 328–342.

Hagan, J & Kay, F. (1995) *Gender in Practice: A Study of Lawyer's Lives* (New York, OUP).

Hanlon, G. (1999) *Lawyers, the State and the Market: Professionalism Revisited* (London, Macmillan).

International Association of Women Judges. (2006) The appointment and removal of judges: independence and diversity (*International Association of Women Judges 8th Biennial Conference*, May 2006, Sydney, Australia).

Iyer, S. (2013) The fleeting benefits of appointments commissions for judicial gender equity, *Commonwealth and Comparative Politics*, 51(1), pp. 97–121.

Jacobs, D. (2014) At law firms, mommy track still holds women back, *Forbes*. Available at: http://www.forbes.com/sites/deborahljacobs/2014/08/05/at-law-firms-mommy-track-still-holds-women-back/#5b9e8678259f, accessed 2 February 2017.

Judiciary NI. (2019) *Judiciary of Northern Ireland*. Available at: https://www.judiciary-ni.gov.uk/about-judiciary/judicial-members, accessed 18 January 2019.

Law Institute of Victoria and Victorian Women Lawyers. (2006) *Bendable or Expendable? Practices and Attitudes Towards Work Flexibility in Victoria's Biggest Legal Employers* (Melbourne, Law Institute of Victoria and Victorian Women Lawyers).

Law Society of Northern Ireland. (2019). Available at: https://www.lawsoc-ni.org/about-us, accessed 18 January 2019.

Leith, P., Dickson, B., Morison, J., Wheeler, S. & Lynch, M. (2013) *Rewarding Merit in Judicial Appointments? A Research Project Undertaken by the School of Law, Queen's University Belfast for the Northern Ireland Judicial Appointments Commission*. Available at: https://pure.qub.ac.uk/ws/files/16480169/NijacReportJan16_1_.pdf, accessed 16 January 2018.

Lord Neuberger (2017) Annual oral evidence taken on 29 March 2017 (Session 2016-17) Q10 (Lord Neuberger of Abbotsbury).

Mack, K. & Roach Anleu, S. (2014) Job satisfaction in the judiciary, *Work Employment and Society*, 28(5), pp. 683–701.

Malleson, K. (2006) Rethinking the merit principle in judicial selection, *Journal of Law and Society*, 33, pp. 126–140.

Marlow, S., Henry, C. & Carter, S. (2009) Exploring the impact of gender upon women's business ownership, *International Small Business Journal*, 27(2), pp. 139–148.

McCarl Nielsen, J. (1990) *Feminist Research Methods: Exemplary Readings in the Social Sciences* (Boulder, Westview Press).

McLoughlin, K. (2015) A particular disappointment? Judging women and the High Court of Australia, *Feminist Legal Studies*, 23(3), pp. 273–294.

Mohr, T. (2014) Why women don't apply for jobs unless they're 100% qualified, *Harvard Business Review*, 25 August. Available at: https://hbr.org/2014/08/why-women-dont-apply-for-jobs-unless-theyre-100-qualified, accessed 18 September 2016.

Morison, J. (2015) Finding "merit" in judicial appointments: the Northern Ireland judicial appointments Commission (NIJAC) and the search for a new judiciary for Northern Ireland, in: A. McAlinden & C. Dwyer (Eds) *Criminal Justice in Transition: The Northern Ireland Context* (Oxford, Hart Publishing), pp. 131–156.

Morison, J. & Dickson, B. (2019) Barriers to High Court appointments in Northern Ireland: a report for the Northern Ireland Judicial Appointments Commission (June 2019).

NISRA. (2017) *NISRA Statistical Bulletin*. Available at: https://www.nisra.gov.uk/sites/nisra.gov.uk/files/publications/MYE16-Bulletin.pdf, accessed 20 May 2018.

Pinnington, A. & Jörgen Sandberg, J. (2013) Lawyers' professional careers: increasing women's inclusion in the partnership of law firms, *Gender, Work and Organisation*, 20 (6), pp. 616–631.

Rackley, E. (2013) *Women, Judging and the Judiciary* (Milton Park, Routledge-Cavendish).

Reichman, N. & Sterling, J. (2002) Recasting the brass ring: deconstructing and reconstructing workplace opportunities for women lawyers, *Capital University Law Review*, 29, pp. 923–977.

Simmons, R. (2017) Changes to barrister parental leave rules are "watershed moment" for diversity says Bar Council, *Lawyer 2B*. Available at: https://l2b.thelawyer.com/issues/l2b-online/changes-to-barrister-maternity-leave-rules-are-watershed-moment/, accessed 13 December 2017.

Solberg, R. (2006) Court size and diversity on the bench: the ninth circuit and its sisters, *Arizona Law Review*, 48, pp. 247–266.

Sommerlad, H. & Sanderson, P. (1998) *Gender, Choice and Commitment: Women Solicitors in England and Wales and the Struggle for Equal Status* (London, Ashgate).

SSRB, Annual Report (2017). Review body on Senior Salaries, Thirty-ninth annual report on Senior Salaries 2017, Cm 9455, July 2017. Available at: https://www.gov.uk/government/uploads/system/uploads/attachment_data/file/629679/SSRB_2017_report_Print.pdf.

Sterling, J. (2016) Overlooked and undervalued: women in private law practice, *Annual Review of Law and Social Science*, 12, pp. 373–393.

The Guardian (2011) *The Law of Motherhood* (28 April). Available at: https://www.theguardian.com/law/2011/apr/28/barristers-solicitors, accessed 13 December 2017.

Thornton, M. (2007) Otherness on the bench: how merit is gendered, *Sydney Law Review*, 29 (3), pp. 391–413.

Turenne, J and Bell, S. (2018) The attractiveness of judicial appointments in the United Kingdom: report to the Senior Salaries Review Body (January 2018) Available at: https://assets.publishing.service.gov.uk/government/uploads/system/uploads/attachment_data/file/748580/SSRB_Report_Attractiveness_Turenne-Bell_Revised_14_March_FINAL_-_temp_pdf.pdf, accessed 18 January 2019.

Twenge, J. (2010) A review of the empirical evidence on generational differences in work attitudes, *Journal of Business Psychology*, 25(2), pp. 201–210.

Valdini, M. & Shortell, C. (2016) Women's representation in the highest court, *Political Research Quarterly*, 69(4), pp. 856–876.

Wald, E. (2010) Symposium: the economic downturn and the legal profession, *Fordham Law Review*, 78(5), pp. 2051–2066.

Walsh, J. (2013) Gender, the work-life interface and wellbeing: a study of hospital doctors, *Gender, Work and Organisation*, 20(4), pp. 439–453.

Welter, F. & Smallbone, D. (2008) Women's entrepreneurship from an institutional perspective: the case of Uzbekistan, *International Entrepreneurship and Management Journal*, 4 (4), pp. 505–520.

Williams, J. & Calvert, C. (2002) Balanced hours: effective part time policies for Washington law firms: the project for attorney retention, *William and Mary Journal of Women and the Law*, 8(3), pp. 357–441.

Wilson, F. (2003) *Organisational Behaviour and Gender* (Oxon, Ashgate Publishing).

Witz, A. (1991), *Professions and Patriarchy* (London, Routledge).

Index

Page numbers in **bold** refer to tables and those in *italic* refer to figures.